HOW TO OPEN A BED AND BREAKFAST BUSINESS

Turn Your Dream into a Successful Inn

Jeanelle K. Douglas

Copyright © 2024 by Jeanelle K. Douglas. All rights reserved. No part of this book, HOW TO OPEN A BED AND BREAKFAST BUSINESS, may be reproduced, stored in a retrieval system, or transmitted in any form or by any means, electronic, mechanical, photocopying, recording, or otherwise, without the prior written permission of the author, Jeanelle K. Douglas.

Table of Contents

Introduction 8

    Welcome to the World of Bed & Breakfast 11

    Why open a bed and breakfast 13

    Overview of the Book 17

Chapter 1 22

    Understanding the bed and breakfast industry 22

    Evolution and Trends in the B&B Industry 24

    Current Market Analysis and Opportunities 28

    Opportunities in the Bed and Breakfast Industry 30

    Competitor Analysis: Knowing Your Niche 32

Chapter 2 36

    Defining Your Vision and Business Plan 36

    Creating your business plan 38

    Budgeting and Financial Planning 41

Chapter 3 45

    Legal Considerations and Regulations 45

    Choosing the Right Legal Structure 50

Factors to Consider 54

Licensing and Permits for B&B Operations 56

Understanding Zoning and Land Use Regulations 60

Chapter 4 64

Location 64

Consideration on accessibility and facilities of the B&B location 69

Navigating real estate and lease agreements 72

Designing and decorating your bed and breakfast (B&B) 76

Interior design trends 79

Sourcing furniture, décor, and amenities for your bed and breakfast (B&B) 84

Chapter 5 88

Marketing and Branding 88

Managing operations 99

Recruiting and Training of Employee 103

Implementing Reservation Systems 106

Exceptional customer service 110

- Maintaining a competitive 113
- Staying Current on Industry Trends 117
- Incorporating sustainable Practices 121
- Seeking feedback 125

Chapter 6 130
- Financial management and revenue optimization 130
- Pricing Strategies 135
- Overhead Management 139
- Diversifying Revenue 144
- Excellent Guest Experiences 149

Chapter 7 157
- Keeping a competitive edge for your bed and breakfast 157
- Sustainable practices in your bed and breakfast (B&B) operations 161
- Gathering of Feed Back for Improvement 165

Chapter 8 169
- Financial Management and Revenue Optimization 169
- Financial Management 169

Revenue Optimization 171

CREATING EFFICIENT PRICING STRATEGIES . 173

Effective Spending and Overhead Management 177

Diversifying Revenue Streams 181

Providing Excellent Guest Experiences 185

Personalizing Services and Facilities 189

Chapter 9 193

Managing visitor comments 193

Adapting To Industry Developments 196

Embracing technology in bed and breakfast operations 200

Chapter 10 204

Addressing Problems 204

Future Trends and Developments in the Bed And Breakfast Sector 207

Business Plan Template 212

Legal checklist for bed and breakfast (B&B) 215

Resource Directory For Bed And Breakfast (B&B) Owners 219

Associations 219

Suppliers 220

Support Services 222

Terms and Meanings Relating To the Bed And Breakfast (B&B) Industry 224

Introduction

Welcome to the fascinating world of bed and breakfasts (B&Bs), where each visit is a one-of-a-kind trip filled with warmth, comfort, and unforgettable memories. Whether you're a seasoned entrepreneur with a love for hospitality or an ambitious innkeeper looking for a new adventure, this book is your vital guide to unlocking the doors to success in the bed and breakfast market.

In recent years, the travel and lodging landscape has changed dramatically. Amidst the ever-changing trends and preferences of modern travelers, bed and breakfasts have emerged as cherished havens that provide more than just a place to rest your head—they provide a sanctuary where guests can immerse themselves in the rich tapestry of local culture, savor homemade breakfast delights, and form meaningful connections with fellow travelers and hosts. But what distinguishes a bed and breakfast from other hotel options?

The personal touch, attention to detail, and genuine hospitality are what define a bed and breakfast experience. From small rural cottages set among rolling hills to ancient metropolitan palaces steeped in charm and elegance, each bed and breakfast has its own particular personality and fascination.

In this book, we'll take a thorough look at the complex world of bed and breakfast ownership, from the initial spark of an idea to the thrilling moment when you greet your first visitors through the door. Whether you want to transform a historic home into a timeless hideaway or add a modern touch to a modest cottage, we will provide you with the expertise, skills, and ideas that is needed to make this happen. Throughout these pages, you'll find essential guidance from experienced innkeepers, industry experts, and successful entrepreneurs who have walked the rewarding route of bed and breakfast ownership.

Each chapter aims to equip you with practical tactics, insider insights, and concrete measures to guide you towards success by negotiating the legal complexities of permits and zoning rules and mastering the art of producing amazing guest experiences. Beyond the practicalities of running a bed and breakfast, this book celebrates the joy, passion, and profound feeling of fulfilment that comes from welcoming visitors into your home and creating cherished experiences that will last a lifetime. It's a monument to the inexhaustible ingenuity, resilience, and steadfast commitment of innkeepers who pour their hearts and souls into every part of their bed and breakfast, making it into a treasured haven for visitors from all over the world.

So, whether you're embarking on this journey as a daring new adventure or the realization of a lifelong dream, I invite you to delve into the pages of this book and discover the extraordinary world of bed and breakfasts—a world where every day is an opportunity to create magic, forge connections, and make a difference in the lives of those who pass through your door. Explore the enchanting realm of bed and breakfasts, where every visit holds a unique story and each guest contributes to your journey.

Welcome to the World of Bed & Breakfast

Welcome, dear reader, to the enchanted world of bed and breakfasts (B&Bs), where hospitality meets home and every visit is a story waiting to happen. This thriving business offers a trip filled with warmth, charm, and limitless possibilities, where personal relationships are valued above all else, and each inn is as distinctive as the people who manage it. As you read this book, you will learn the keys to unlocking the doors of your own bed and breakfast, allowing you to create amazing experiences for your visitors and leave an everlasting impression on their memory.

But first, let us build a realistic picture of what you may expect in this enthralling realm. Consider a beautiful Victorian estate hidden among rolling hills, its front porch furnished with rocking rockers encouraging guests to relax and rest. Imagine a charming cabin by the sea, where the salty wind speaks of adventure and peace.

A rustic farmhouse surrounded by acres of rich land serves farm-to-table meals alongside real hospitality. These are just a few examples of the rich tapestry that is the world of bed and breakfasts. From ancient estates to sophisticated urban getaways, tiny hideaways to large rural inns, each B&B has its own distinct appeal and attraction, offering guests a break from the mundane and a look into the heart of hospitality. Aside from their architectural splendor and picturesque locations, what truly distinguishes bed and breakfasts is the personal touch of their hosts. Owners of B&Bs imbue their establishments with warmth and personality, opening their doors to provide lodging and welcome guests into their homes and lives.

In the following chapters, we will dig deeply into the art and science of starting and operating a successful bed and breakfast. From developing a compelling vision and business plan to navigating legalities, constructing welcoming locations, and mastering the intricacies of the guest experience, we will provide you with the information and resources you need to make your goal of owning a bed and breakfast a reality.

So, whether you're a seasoned innkeeper trying to rejuvenate your property or an ambitious entrepreneur searching for a new adventure, join us as we explore the limitless possibilities that exist in the world of bed and breakfasts. Let's work together to open the door to your own slice of hospitality heaven and provide wonderful experiences for tourists from all around. Welcome to the trip of a lifetime.

Why open a bed and breakfast

Starting a bed and breakfast (B&B) is more than simply a commercial enterprise; it's a vocation, a passion, and a lifestyle. But what really draws people to owning and managing a bed and breakfast?

Let's look at some of the reasons why people choose to work in this unique and lucrative industry:

1. Personal Fulfillment: The desire to make meaningful relationships and enhance the lives of others is at the core of every successful bed and breakfast. As a bed and breakfast owner, you will have the chance to welcome guests from all walks of life into your house, sharing tales, laughter, and unique experiences along the way. The sense of

accomplishment that comes with creating a warm, welcoming environment in which guests feel like family is unsurpassed.

2. Creative expression: Owning a bed and breakfast is like being the curator of your own artistic creation. From constructing attractive guest rooms to creating delectable breakfast menus, every facet of your B&B allows you to show your distinct personality and style. Whether you have an eye for interior design, a passion for culinary delights, or a talent for creating unique experiences, a bed and breakfast is the ideal setting for your creativity to blossom.

3. Flexibility and Freedom: Unlike regular 9-to-5 occupations, operating a B&B provides a degree of flexibility and independence that many budding entrepreneurs value. As your own boss, you have the freedom to choose your own schedule, prioritize your personal and professional obligations, and adjust your business to your lifestyle needs. Whether you choose to spend your days gardening in the sunlight or visiting local sites with your guests, running a bed and breakfast allows you to achieve the ideal balance between work and leisure.

4. Financial Opportunity: While passion and creativity are the motivating elements behind many B&B enterprises, the financial prospects in the market should also be considered. With the increase in experience travel and a growing desire for unique lodging alternatives, the bed and breakfast business provides a profitable potential for entrepreneurs wishing to profit from the hospitality market. From luring visitors looking for rich cultural experiences to organizing weddings, retreats, and special events, clever B&B operators may generate a variety of revenue streams.

5. Community Engagement: Bed and breakfasts play an important role in creating a sense of community and sustaining local economies. By highlighting your destination's particular attractions and cooperating with local craftsmen, farmers, and businesses, you not only help your community's economic prosperity but also become an important part of its cultural fabric. From identifying hidden treasures and off-the-beaten-path attractions to supporting neighborhood projects and events, running a bed and breakfast allows you to become a respected member of your community and helping the people around you.

In essence, the choice to open a bed and breakfast stems from a love of hospitality, a desire for creative expression, and a need for personal and professional satisfaction. Running a bed and breakfast offers a rewarding path that includes adventure, development, and limitless possibilities, whether you're attracted to creating amazing guest experiences, the independence of being your own boss, or the ability to make a significant contribution to your community.

Overview of the Book

In this thorough book, we will take you on a tour through the complicated world of bed and breakfasts (B&Bs), covering every facet of starting and running a successful operation in today's changing hospitality market. Whether you're a seasoned innkeeper trying to rejuvenate your property or an ambitious entrepreneur dreaming of a new adventure, this book will help you realize your vision and provide exceptional experiences for your guests.

We begin by looking at the development, trends, and current market analysis of the B&B business. By identifying niche prospects and performing competition analysis, we offer vital insights into the business environment and assist you in determining your distinctive market positioning. Developing a compelling vision and detailed business plan is critical for laying the groundwork for your B&B operation.

We walk you through the process of articulating your vision, setting realistic goals, and creating a strategic roadmap that will lead you to success. Navigating the legal environment of the hotel sector can be difficult, but it is critical for maintaining compliance and preserving your investment.

From selecting the appropriate legal structure to getting the essential permissions and licenses, we provide you with the knowledge and tools you need to manage the legalities of starting and maintaining a bed and breakfast.

The location of your B&B may make or break your business, so selecting the correct location is crucial. We go over the aspects to consider when considering possible locations, from accessibility and amenities to zoning rules and real estate issues, to help you choose the ideal setting for your B&B. Creating a pleasant and appealing setting is critical for delivering unforgettable visitor experiences. From interior design trends to sourcing furniture and décor, we offer practical advice and inspiration for creating and equipping your bed and breakfast to reflect your own style and personality.

In today's competitive economy, efficient marketing and branding are critical to attracting guests and distinguishing yourself in the marketplace. We look at ways to establish your brand identity, create a marketing strategy, and use online and offline channels to reach your target demographic and increase bookings. Efficient operations are vital for providing outstanding visitor experiences while increasing profitability.

From hiring and training employees to installing reservation systems and delivering excellent customer service, we cover all of the elements of running a successful bed and breakfast. Staying ahead of the curve is critical to success in the fast-paced hospitality sector. We investigate techniques for remaining current with industry trends, implementing sustainable practices, and constantly innovating to preserve a competitive advantage in the market. Effective financial management is critical to the long-term viability of your B&B.

We discuss pricing tactics, spending management, and income stream diversification in order to maximize profitability and maintain your company's financial stability.

Every successful bed and breakfast has a dedication to offering great guest experiences. From providing unique touches to dealing with visitor comments and reviews, we look at how to delight your guests and ensure they leave with great memories. The hospitality sector is continuously developing, and remaining adaptive is critical to success. We look at the most recent developments and innovations in the B&B sector and talk about how to adapt to market changes and future-proof your business for long-term success. As we come to the end of our voyage, we reflect on the lessons learned and the adventures ahead. This last chapter provides final insights and success recommendations, allowing you to confidently and excitedly begin your own B&B experience.

The appendix contains useful tools for your B&B journey, such as sample business plan templates, legal checklists, and a database of associations, suppliers, and support services. The glossary compiles key terminology and meanings from throughout the text for easy reference and clarification. In conclusion, this book offers a thorough guide for anybody who wants to create and run a profitable bed and breakfast. Whether you're a seasoned innkeeper or a first-time entrepreneur, join us on this adventure as we uncover the keys to success in the fascinating world of bed and breakfasts.

Chapter 1

Understanding the bed and breakfast industry

To begin the process of founding and maintaining a successful bed and breakfast (B&B), it is critical to have a thorough awareness of the industry environment. The bed and breakfast industry is a dynamic and expanding segment of the larger hotel industry, distinguished by its unusual combination of personalized service, intimate accommodations, and distinctive visitor experiences.

The bed and breakfast industry is fundamentally based on hospitality traditions and the art of delivering memorable stays for guests seeking a more personal and genuine hotel experience. Unlike regular hotels, which sometimes promote uniform facilities and formal service, bed and breakfasts allow visitors to engage with local culture, immerse themselves in lovely settings, and get customized attention from their hosts. One of the distinguishing features of the B&B sector is its wide range of properties, each with its own distinct ambiance, facilities, and guest experiences.

From ancient mansions and quaint cottages to sophisticated urban getaways and rural farmhouses, B&Bs come in many shapes and sizes, catering to a diverse variety of tourist tastes and interests. The bed & breakfast sector has grown and transformed significantly in recent years, owing to changes in customer tastes, technological improvements, and growing travel habits.

Today's tourists are increasingly looking for unique and original experiences that allow them to interact with local culture, get individual treatment, and avoid typical hotel rooms. As a result, B&B owners are always inventing and adapting to suit the changing demands and expectations of their customers. To stay ahead in a competitive market, B&Bs are adopting new trends and tactics, such as implementing sustainable practices and offering immersive packages, as well as employing technology to enhance guest experiences and streamline operations.

Furthermore, the bed and breakfast sector contributes significantly to local economies and tourism promotion in towns all over the world. B&Bs help their towns' economic growth and cultural vibrancy by highlighting the distinctive attractions of their destinations, cooperating with local craftsmen and companies, and giving customized advice and insights to visitors. In the following chapters, we will dig deeper into the subtleties of the bed and breakfast sector, investigating current market trends, identifying specialized prospects, and giving practical insights and methods for aspiring B&B operators.

Whether you're a seasoned innkeeper trying to rebrand your property or an ambitious entrepreneur looking to break into the hospitality industry, this book will provide you with the knowledge and skills you need to thrive in the fascinating and rewarding world of bed and breakfasts.

Evolution and Trends in the B&B Industry

The bed and breakfast (B&B) sector has evolved dramatically throughout the years, influenced by changing visitor tastes, technological improvements, and increasing customer needs. From its humble beginnings as family-owned guesthouses to its current standing as a thriving section of the hospitality business, the bed and breakfast industry has constantly changed and developed to meet the expectations of modern travelers.

Let's look at how the B&B sector has evolved and what trends are currently affecting it.

Evolution of the Bed and Breakfast Industry: Travelers in the middle Ages sought refuge and hospitality in private houses in Europe, tracing the origins of the contemporary bed and breakfast.

In the United States, the notion became popular in the nineteenth century, when inns and boarding houses provided lodging for tourists touring the countryside and visiting small communities.

However, it wasn't until the late twentieth century that the bed and breakfast sector saw a renaissance, fueled by tourists' rising need for customized experiences and honest encounters.

The emergence of the sharing economy and internet booking platforms has driven the expansion of the bed and breakfast business, making it simpler for homeowners to welcome guests and for tourists to find new lodging alternatives.

1. Personalization and authenticity are two trends in the B&B industry. Today's vacationers seek genuine experiences that go beyond generic motels. B&Bs provide individualized hospitality, allowing tourists to interact with local hosts, immerse themselves in the community, and get authentic hospitality that represents the destination's culture and tradition.

2. Unique and Boutique Experiences: Bed and breakfasts come in different shapes and sizes, from historic mansions and charming cottages to eco-friendly getaways and urban sanctuaries. The drive toward distinctive and boutique experiences has resulted in a profusion of themed bed and breakfasts that cater to certain niches, such as culinary-focused inns, wine region getaways, and pet-friendly lodgings.

3. Technical Integration: Many bed and breakfasts are incorporating technology to enhance the visitor experience,

while still maintaining their old-world charm and friendliness. From online booking platforms and smartphone check-in to smart house amenities and tailored concierge services, B&Bs are finding new ways to incorporate technology while retaining their distinct charm.

4. Sustainable and Environmentally Friendly Practices: With increasing awareness of environmental sustainability, many bed and breakfasts are implementing eco-friendly methods to reduce their carbon footprint and attract eco-conscious guests. Sustainability has emerged as a major trend in the bed and breakfast sector, encompassing everything from energy-efficient improvements and locally sourced amenities to trash reduction programs and green certification.

5. Social and Digital Marketing: B&Bs are using social media and digital marketing platforms to promote their unique offers, interact with guests, and attract new customers. Instagram and Pinterest have evolved into strong tools for bed and breakfasts to exhibit their property's aesthetics, share guest experiences, and connect with tourists looking for ideas for their next holiday.

6. Experienced Travel: Today's tourists expect engaging experiences that will leave them with long-lasting memories, not just a place to rest. B&Bs are capitalizing on this trend by providing experience packages and activities that extend beyond lodging, such as cooking courses, wine tastings, farm-to-table dining experiences, and guided tours of local landmarks.

Current Market Analysis and Opportunities

As of now, the bed and breakfast (B&B) industry is a thriving and robust part of the overall hospitality economy. Despite the challenges provided by global events such as the COVID-19 epidemic, the bed and breakfast business has exhibited amazing adaptation and durability, providing several opportunities for ambitious innkeepers and entrepreneurs.

Let's take a look at the current market analysis and potential for the B&B industry:

1. Recovery and Resilience: Following the disruptions caused by the COVID-19 epidemic, the bed and breakfast industry is showing signs of recovery and resilience. As travel restrictions loosen and consumer confidence gradually recovers, there is an increase in demand for domestic and regional travel, with many passengers looking for secure and isolated accommodations away from popular tourist regions.

2. Changes in Travel Preferences: The epidemic has caused a shift in travel tastes, with passengers valuing safety, privacy, and authenticity. B&Bs, with their private and customized hospitality, are well-positioned to address these changing expectations, providing visitors with a secure and quiet hideaway where they can engage in authentic and engaging travel experiences.

3. Workation and Staycation Trends Rise: With remote work becoming more common, many travelers are adopting the concepts of "workations" and "staycations," looking for lodging alternatives that combine work, pleasure, and relaxation. B&Bs, with their friendly and homey ambiance, are great for tourists seeking to mix business and pleasure in a relaxing and stimulating environment.

4. Focus on Local and Experiential Travel: Local and experiential travel are becoming increasingly popular, with tourists seeking authentic and engaging encounters that link them to the destination's culture, tradition, and community. B&Bs, which are typically located in gorgeous and off-the-beaten-path areas, allow tourists to discover hidden gems, engage with locals, and immerse themselves in the destination's own character.

Opportunities in the Bed and Breakfast Industry

1. Niche or Specialty Markets: B&B owners can cater to a variety of niche and specialist markets, including eco-friendly getaways, wellness-focused inns, pet-friendly lodgings, and themed B&Bs based on certain interests and hobbies. B&B owners can differentiate their facilities and win loyal customers.

2. Digital Innovation and Technology Integration: Bed and breakfasts may use digital innovation and technology

integration to improve the guest experience, streamline operations, and reach a larger audience. Embracing technology, from integrating online booking systems and mobile check-in services to harnessing social media for marketing and guest engagement, may help bed and breakfasts remain competitive in today's digital economy.

3. Sustainable and Responsible Tourism With rising awareness of environmental sustainability, there is a greater need for sustainable and ethical tourist activities. B&Bs may adopt eco-friendly initiatives such as energy-efficient improvements, trash reduction programs, locally sourced amenities, and green certifications, which will appeal to eco-conscious tourists while also aligning with sustainable tourism objectives.

4. Cooperation and Partnership: B&B owners can look into cooperation and partnership options with local companies, craftsmen, and attractions to create unique guest experiences and expand their property's services. By forming strategic connections with local wineries, restaurants, tour operators, and cultural groups, B&Bs may provide visitors with

personalized experiences that showcase the destination's inherent character and attractiveness.

5. Adaptivity and Flexibility: As the tourism industry evolves, B&B operators must stay adaptive and agile in order to respond to changing client tastes and market trends. Whether it's implementing flexible booking regulations, offering bespoke packages, or diversifying income sources with extra services and activities, adaptation is essential for prospering in the competitive B&B market.

Competitor Analysis: Knowing Your Niche

Understanding your competition is critical to success in the bed and breakfast (B&B) market. Conducting a thorough competition study enables you to establish your niche, differentiate your property, and profit from market trends.

Here's how to do a detailed competition study to help you carve out your niche in the bed and breakfast industry:

1. Identify your rivals: Start by finding direct rivals in your area. These are additional B&Bs that provide comparable rooms and services to a similar guest population. Use internet travel platforms, review websites, and local directories to create a list of competing B&Bs in your desired region. Consider indirect rivals like boutique hotels, vacation rentals, and regular accommodation choices, which may cater to a similar client group.

2. Evaluate Their Offers: Compare the amenities, services, and experiences provided by your competition. This comprises hotel choices, breakfast selections, amenities (such as spa treatments, guided tours, or recreational activities), and any distinguishing features.

Assess your rivals' pricing methods, such as accommodation rates, seasonal discounts, and package packages.

Pay attention to guest evaluations and feedback to determine what they appreciate most about your rivals' products.

3. Understanding their target audience:

Determine which target audience(s) your rivals are catering to. This includes age, income, interests, and travel preferences.

Consider the different visitor groups' individual demands and preferences, as well as how your hotel might differentiate itself to appeal to certain target audiences.

4. Evaluate their branding and marketing strategies:

Evaluate your rivals' branding and marketing efforts, including their website design, branding components, messaging, and online presence.

Examine their social media platforms, blog articles, email marketing campaigns, and other promotional activities to see how they interact with potential guests and generate reservations.

5. Determine if there are any gaps or possibilities in their marketing strategy that you can use to differentiate your property.

Assess each competitor's strengths and shortcomings, including location, property size, facilities, guest experience, customer service, and reputation.

Consider how your property may use its strengths to outperform competitors while addressing any deficiencies to strengthen its competitive position.

6. Differentiate Your Property:

Using your information, discover possibilities to differentiate your home and carve out a niche in the market.

7. Consider unique selling points (USPs) that distinguish your resort from rivals, such as themed rooms, customized services, environmentally responsible initiatives, or tailored guest experiences.

8. Create a compelling value proposition that speaks to your target audience and clearly illustrates the advantages of selecting your B&B over rivals.

Chapter 2

Defining Your Vision and Business Plan

Creating a clear vision and detailed business strategy is critical for laying the groundwork for your bed and breakfast (B&B) enterprise. Your vision guides the identity and direction of your B&B, while your business plan gives a road map for attaining your objectives and guaranteeing long-term success. Here's how you can articulate your goal and create a strong business strategy for your bed and breakfast:

1. Reflect on Your Purpose: Begin by thinking about your own reasons and goals for running a B&B. What motivated you to join the hospitality industry? What values and beliefs would you like your B&B to embody? Your vision should show your enthusiasm for hospitality and dedication to providing memorable visitor experiences.

2. Imagine your ideal bed and breakfast: Imagine your dream bed and breakfast, as well as the experience you want to provide for your visitors. Consider the property's location, architectural style, mood, facilities, and the sort of guests you hope to attract. Visualize the distinct atmosphere and character that will distinguish your B&B from rivals.

3. **Clarify Your Goals:** Define precise, measurable goals that align with your B&B vision. These objectives might include aims for occupancy rates, revenue growth, guest satisfaction ratings, sustainability efforts, and community participation. Setting specific goals helps provide you with focus and direction while you create your company strategy.

4. **Define Your Target Market:** Determine your target market(s) using demographic information such as age, income level, interests, and travel preferences. Consider your potential visitors' wants and preferences, as well as how your B&B may accommodate their special wishes, such as a romantic retreat for couples, a family-friendly break, or a wellness retreat for health-conscious tourists.

5. **Describe Your Unique Selling Proposition (USP):** Determine what distinguishes your B&B from rivals and create your unique selling proposition (USP). This might include everything from your property's unique features and facilities to personalized guest services, eco-friendly efforts, or themed events. Your unique selling point should explain

the value proposition that makes your bed and breakfast appealing to your target market.

Creating your business plan

1. **Executive Summary:** Give a brief summary of your bed and breakfast operation, including your vision, goals, target market, unique selling point, and essential parts of your business strategy.

2. **Business description:** Describe your B&B in depth, including its location, size, architectural style, facilities, services, and distinguishing characteristics. Discuss your target market(s) and how your B&B caters to their requirements and preferences.

3. **Market Analysis:** Conduct detailed research on the B&B industry, including market trends, consumer demographics, the competitive environment, and potential growth areas. Identify market gaps that your B&B can fill and profit from.

4. **Marketing and Sales Strategy:** Describe your marketing and sales strategies for attracting guests and increasing reservations. This might involve digital marketing approaches, social media participation, collaborations with local companies, promotions, and price strategies.

5. **Operations Plan:** Describe your bed and breakfast's day-to-day operations, including personnel needs, reservation systems, housekeeping processes, guest services, and quality control methods. Consider how you'll provide outstanding visitor experiences while being operationally efficient.

6. **Financial estimates:** Create financial estimates for your B&B, such as starting costs, revenue forecasts, spending budgets, and cash flow projections. This will help you determine your enterprise's financial feasibility and secure financing if necessary.

7. **Risk Management:** Identify possible risks and obstacles to your bed and breakfast business, such as economic downturns, seasonal swings, regulatory changes, or unanticipated catastrophes like natural disasters or

pandemics. Create ways to manage these risks while ensuring company continuity.

8. Sustainability and Social Responsibility: Explain your dedication to sustainability and social responsibility, including actions to lessen your environmental footprint, help local communities, and have a good social effect.

9. Implementation strategy: Outline the procedures necessary to carry out your business strategy, including dates, milestones, responsibilities, and resources. Establish metrics to track progress and alter your plan as needed.

Crafting a detailed business plan for your bed and breakfast can lay a firm foundation for success and boost your chances of meeting your objectives in the competitive hospitality sector. Your business plan will serve as a road map for establishing and managing your bed and breakfast, guiding your decisions and actions as you bring your vision to life and provide unforgettable experiences for your visitors.

Budgeting and Financial Planning

Budgeting and financial planning are essential for launching and running a successful bed and breakfast (B&B) business. Proper budgeting allows you to properly allocate resources, control costs, and guarantee the financial health of your B&B.

Here's how to do budgeting and financial planning for your bed and breakfast:

1. **Initial Expenditures:** Identify all one-time initial expenditures for starting your bed and breakfast, such as: Identify all one-time initial expenses for starting your bed and breakfast, such as: Property acquisition or leasing expenses, Renovations and interior design, furniture, fixtures, and equipment, Licenses and permissions, Marketing and branding expenditures, Legal and professional costs, Initial inventory and supplies.

   Create a precise budget worksheet that breaks out each starting cost and predicts the associated expenditures.

2. **Operating Expenses:**
Calculate your continuing running expenditures, which include: Rent or mortgage payments, Utilities: electricity, water, gas, and internet, Insurance (property, liability, and business interruption), property upkeep and repairs, Employee pay and perks, Marketing and advertising expenses, Property management costs (if any) Guest amenities and supplies, Administrative expenses (office supplies and software subscriptions), Estimate each expense category using market research, industry benchmarks, and projected occupancy rates.

3. **Revenue Projections:** Establish revenue projections based on occupancy rates, average daily rates (ADRs), and RevPAR.

Consider seasonal demand fluctuations and adjust your revenue projections accordingly.

Consider additional revenue streams like food and beverage sales, event hosting, and ancillary services.

4. **Cash Flow Management:** Create a cash flow projection to track cash in and out of your B&B business. Plan for periods of positive and negative

cash flow to ensure you have enough liquidity to cover expenses in lean months.

Implement cash flow-improving strategies, such as offering discounts for early bookings or providing guests with flexible payment terms.

5. **Contingency Planning:** Establish a fund to cover unexpected expenses or emergencies, such as equipment breakdowns, property damage, or economic downturns.

Aim to set aside a percentage of your monthly revenue to create a financial buffer.

6. **Pricing Strategy:** Create a pricing strategy that aligns with your revenue goals, market demand, and guest expectations.

Research competitor pricing and adjust your rates accordingly to stay competitive while remaining profitable.

To attract guests and maximize revenue, consider offering special promotions, packages, or discounts during off-peak hours.

7. **Financial Management Tools:** Use accounting software, budgeting apps, or spreadsheets to track

expenses, manage cash flow, and analyze financial performance.

Review your financial reports and metrics on a regular basis to identify cost-cutting opportunities, revenue optimization, and business growth.

8. **Monitoring and Review:** Hold regular financial review meetings to evaluate your B&B's financial performance, compare actual results to budgeted projections, and make necessary adjustments.

Monitor key performance indicators (KPIs) such as occupancy rates, average daily rates, revenue per available room, and profitability ratios to assess the health of your B&B.

9. **Professional Advice:** Consult with financial advisors, accountants, or business consultants who have experience in the hospitality industry to improve your budgeting and planning strategies.

Implementing thorough budgeting and financial planning practices will allow you to effectively manage the financial aspects of your B&B business, maximize revenue, and ensure long-term sustainability and success.

Chapter 3

Legal Considerations and Regulations

Navigating legal concerns and laws is a vital component of opening and running a bed and breakfast (B&B). Compliance with local, state, and federal laws is critical for protecting your B&B, ensuring your guests' safety and well-being, and upholding the integrity of your operations.

Here are some major legal aspects and requirements to be aware of:

1. Zoning and land use regulations:

Check your local zoning statutes and regulations to make sure your property is designated for commercial use as a bed and breakfast. Obtain any permissions or variances required to run a B&B in your region. Ensure that all property-use limitations, occupancy limits, parking requirements, and signage standards are followed.

2. Licenses and Permits:

Obtain the necessary licenses and permissions for operating a bed and breakfast in your jurisdiction.

Common licenses and permissions include business licenses, hotel permits, food service permits (if meals are served), health department permits, and alcohol permits. Renew licenses and permissions as needed, making sure to meet renewal deadlines.

3. Health and Safety Rules: Follow health and safety rules to safeguard the safety of your visitors and staff.

Keep the environment safe and hygienic by adhering to food safety standards, fire safety laws, building codes, and occupancy restrictions. Adhere to adequate hygiene standards, sanitation processes, and routine facility and equipment maintenance.

4. Ensure adequate insurance coverage to protect your B&B from risks and obligations.

Think about policies like property insurance, liability insurance, business interruption insurance, and workers compensation insurance. Carefully review insurance plans to understand coverage limits, exclusions, and deductibles.

5. Employment Laws:

Recognize and follow federal, state, and local employment rules and regulations. Comply with wage and hour rules, such as minimum wage, overtime compensation, and employee categorization (exempt vs. non-exempt).

Keep accurate records of employee hours worked, pay paid, and employment agreements.

6. Taxation and financial reporting:

Learn about the tax duties associated with running a B&B, such as income taxes, sales taxes, and occupancy taxes.

Register for federal and state tax identification numbers when needed, and submit tax returns on time. Keep accurate financial records and follow the correct accounting standards to make tax filing and compliance easier.

7. Accessibility Compliance: Ensure compliance with accessibility rules and regulations, such as the Americans with Disabilities Act (ADA) and state and local accessibility standards. Make special arrangements for disabled people, such as accessible parking, entrances, and lodgings.

8. Data Protection and Privacy: Comply with data protection laws and regulations to safeguard visitor privacy and personal information.

Implement safeguards for guest data, such as secure storage, encryption, and adherence to privacy regulations.

9. Respect Intellectual Property Rights: Do not violate trademarks, copyrights, or other proprietary rights. Obtain permission or a license before using copyrighted content, trademarks, or branding components.

10. Contractual Agreements: Make sure terms and conditions are clear and detailed. Contracts may include agreements with visitors (e.g., terms and conditions, cancellation policies), vendors (e.g., suppliers, service providers), and workers (e.g., employment contracts, non-disclosure agreements).

11. Continuous Compliance and Updates: Stay up-to-date on any changes in laws, regulations, or industry standards that may affect your bed and breakfast business. Policies, procedures, and practices should be reviewed and updated on a regular basis to maintain continued legal compliance.

Seeking legal advice from specialists, such as attorneys who specialize in hospitality law or regulatory compliance, may help you manage the complex environment of legal concerns and laws that apply to running a bed and breakfast business. Understanding and resolving these legal concerns ahead of time will help you safeguard your B&B Company and provide a safe and compliant environment for your visitors.

Choosing the Right Legal Structure

Selecting the appropriate legal structure for your bed and breakfast (B&B) is a critical choice that will affect many areas of your business, including liability, taxation, and management flexibility. When deciding on a legal structure, you must take into account your unique circumstances, long-term goals, and preferences. Here are common legal arrangements for bed and breakfasts, along with aspects to consider for each:

1. Sole Proprietorship: A sole proprietorship is the most basic type of business structure, where the owner and business are regarded as the same legal entity.

Advantages:

- Simple and cost-effective setup and operation.
- Full control over corporate decisions and operations.
- Simplified tax reporting because the owner's personal tax return includes business revenue.

Disadvantages:

- Unrestricted personal accountability for corporate debts and legal duties.
- Limited capacity to obtain funds and attract investors.
- There is no separation between personal and company assets, thereby increasing personal financial risk.

2. Partnership: A partnership is a business form where two or more persons share ownership and responsibilities for the company.

Advantages:

- Partners share management and decision-making responsibilities.
- Partnership arrangements provide extra funds and resources.
- Pass-through taxes, which require partners to record business profits and losses on their personal tax returns.

Disadvantages:

- Unlimited personal accountability for partnership debts and legal duties.
- There is a risk of disagreements and conflicts among partners.
- Shared decision-making can lead to divergent corporate directions and tactics.

3. Limited Liability Company (LLC):

An LLC is a hybrid business form that combines a corporation's limited liability protection with the flexibility and tax benefits of a partnership.

The advantages of an LLC:

- Less personal liability for corporate debts and legal responsibilities, which protect members' personal assets.
- Adjustable management structure and profit distribution.
- Pass-through taxes, which require members to disclose LLC income and losses on their personal tax returns.

Disadvantages:

- More difficult and expensive to form and manage than sole proprietorships and partnerships.
- The annual filing requirements and administrative obligations differ by state.

In comparison to corporations, businesses have a limited opportunity to obtain funds through equity financing.

4. Corporation: A corporation is a separate legal entity from its shareholders, who elect a board of directors to supervise the firm.

Some advantages include

- Limited shareholder liability protection and the separation of personal assets from corporate obligations.
- The ability to raise funds through stock sales and attract investors.
- Perpetual existence, regardless of ownership or administration.

Disadvantages

- More difficult and expensive to form and manage than other legal arrangements.
- Double taxation occurs when business profits are taxed at the corporate level and then paid to shareholders as dividends.
- Formal corporate governance standards, such as yearly meetings, record-keeping, and state regulatory compliance.

Factors to Consider

Liability Protection: Determine the desired amount of personal liability protection for yourself, partners, or investors in the B&B business.

Tax Implications: Consider the tax consequences of each legal structure, such as income taxes, self-employment taxes, and prospective tax breaks.

Management Flexibility: Determine your choices for management structure, decision-making authority, and profit sharing among owners or members.

Cost and Complexity: Consider the initial setup expenses, ongoing maintenance needs, and administrative obligations for each legal structure.

Long-Term Goals: Match your legal structure to your long-term company objectives, such as expansion plans, exit strategies, and succession planning.

Consulting with legal and financial specialists, such as attorneys and accountants who understand small business and hospitality legislation, may help you choose the best legal structure for your bed and breakfast. You can choose the ideal legal structure for your B&B business by carefully evaluating your alternatives and taking into account your organization.

Licensing and Permits for B&B Operations

Licensing and permits are required to legally operate a bed and breakfast (B&B) business and comply with local, state, and federal regulations. Obtaining the necessary licenses and permits demonstrates your commitment to running a safe and reputable business while protecting the interests of your customers and the community. Here are some common licenses and permits required for bed and breakfast operations:

1. Business License: A general business license is typically required to operate any business, including a bed and breakfast, in a specific jurisdiction. Business license requirements vary by location and may be issued by the city, county, or state government.

2. Lodging Permit: Many municipalities require a lodging permit or operating license for establishments that provide overnight accommodations, such as bed and breakfasts. This permit ensures that you follow local safety, zoning, and taxation regulations.

3. Health Department Permit: B&Bs that serve food to guests, such as complimentary breakfasts or other meals, may require a health department permit. Adhering to food safety regulations and sanitation standards protects guests' health.

4. Alcohol Permit (if applicable): If you plan to serve or sell alcohol at your B&B, you may need to obtain an alcohol permit or liquor license from the regulatory agency. The requirements and regulations for alcohol permits vary depending on the jurisdiction.

5. Occupancy Tax Permit: Many localities impose occupancy taxes or transient occupancy taxes on accommodations, including bed and breakfasts. Obtaining an occupancy tax permit allows you to collect and pay taxes to the local government.

6. Building and Zoning Permits: Depending on the extent of your property's renovations or modifications, you may need to obtain building permits from the local building department. Furthermore, zoning permits may be required to ensure that your property follows land use regulations and zoning ordinances.

7. Fire Safety Permit: B&Bs must follow fire safety regulations to protect guests in case of an emergency. This could include obtaining a fire safety permit or adhering to fire code requirements like smoke detectors, fire extinguishers, and emergency exit routes.

8. Signage Permit: If you intend to display signage for your B&B, such as a business name, logo, or directional signs, you may need to obtain a permit from the local zoning or planning department. Signage regulations differ between jurisdictions.

9. Environmental Health Permit (if applicable): Depending on your B&B's location and activities, you may need to obtain permits for water quality, wastewater management, and other environmental regulations.

10. Special Use Permits (if applicable): Some B&Bs may need special use permits for unique features or activities, such as hosting events, providing outdoor recreational activities, or operating in historic districts.

If you plan to operate your B&B on a residential property, you may need to obtain a home occupation permit or variance to comply with local zoning ordinances and regulations on home-based businesses.

It's important to research and understand the specific licensing and permit requirements applicable to your B&B business. Contacting the local government offices, such as the city or county clerk's office, planning department, health department, or business licensing department, can provide valuable guidance and assistance in obtaining the necessary licenses and permits for your B&B operations. Additionally, consulting with legal and regulatory experts familiar with hospitality industry regulations can help ensure compliance and avoid potential issues down the road.

Understanding Zoning and Land Use Regulations

Understanding zoning and land use restrictions is critical for bed and breakfast (B&B) owners to comply with local government regulations and run their companies properly. Zoning rules dictate the utilization of properties in a specific region, encompassing restrictions on commercial operations, residential areas, and mixed-use zones. Here is what B&B proprietors should know about zoning and land use regulations:

1. Zoning Designations: Municipalities split regions into zoning districts, each with its own set of authorized land use and development laws.

Common zoning classifications for B&B enterprises may include residential, commercial, mixed-use, agricultural, or special-purpose zones.

B&B owners should identify the particular zoning designation(s) that apply to their property as well as comprehend the permissible uses and restrictions within that zone.

2. Permitted Uses: Zoning rules define the permitted land uses within each district, such as residential, commercial, industrial, institutional, or recreational.

Depending on municipal restrictions, bed and breakfast enterprises may be authorized in zoning zones designated for residential or mixed-use uses.

B&B owners should consult their local zoning code to see if operating a B&B is a permissible land use within their property's zoning classification.

3. Conditional Use Permits (CUPs) or Special Use Permits (SUPs): B&B businesses may need a conditional use permit (CUP) or special use permit (SUP) to operate in a zoning district if it is not an allowed land use by right. Obtaining a CUP or SUP often requires a public review procedure, which may include hearings before the local planning commission or zoning board as well as showing compliance with particular criteria and requirements.

4. Regulations for Home-Based Businesses: Bed and breakfast operators who operate from a domestic residence may be subject to additional home-based business requirements.

Home occupation licenses or variances may be necessary to assure compliance with local zoning statutes and regulations that regulate home-based companies, such as signs, parking, noise, and guest accommodations.

5. Parking and Traffic Consideration: Zoning rules may include limitations for off-street parking, loading and unloading places, and traffic circulation in order to meet the demands of visitors while minimizing impacts on adjacent properties.

B&B operators should be aware of parking restrictions and plan how they will supply enough parking for visitors while adhering to zoning laws.

6. Height and Setback Restrictions: Zoning rules may have setback requirements that specify the distance between buildings and property borders, as well as height limitations that limit the height of structures.

When constructing or renovating buildings or structures on their land, B&B owners must guarantee that the setback and height rules are followed.

7. Regulations for Historic Districts: B&B properties in historic districts may be subject to extra rules and design criteria to preserve the area's historic character and architectural integrity.

B&B owners should become aware of any historic district restrictions and secure any appropriate approvals or permits for restorations or improvements to their property.

8. The Compliance and Permitting Procedure: B&B owners should examine the zoning code, land use rules, and permitting process that apply to their property.

Consultation with local planning department officials or zoning administrators can provide information on zoning restrictions, permit requirements, and the application procedure for establishing a bed and breakfast.

B&B operators must understand zoning and land use restrictions in order to comply with local government requirements and run their companies legally.

Chapter 4

Location

Choosing the correct location for your bed and breakfast (B&B) is an important choice that will affect many elements of your business.

When considering prospective sites for your bed and breakfast (B&B), it's critical to look into several criteria to ensure you make an informed selection that corresponds with your company's aims and vision.

Here's a more extensive analysis of each factor:

1. Evaluate prospective sites based on your target market's demographics, interests, and preferences. For example, if your bed and breakfast caters to couples looking for a romantic trip, you could select a position near picturesque areas, wineries, or cultural activities. Understanding your target market's tastes will allow you to select a venue that will appeal to your prospective guests.

2. Accessibility: Evaluate possible sites' transportation choices and closeness to essential destinations. A suitable

position near major transportation hubs, airports, or highways may attract customers who value ease of movement. Furthermore, proximity to tourist attractions, outdoor recreational areas, food alternatives, and entertainment venues might make your bed and breakfast more appealing to potential visitors.

3. Neighborhood Characteristics and Surroundings:

Examine the qualities of the area and surroundings to verify that they match the mood and vibe you wish to create for your B&B. Consider safety, attractiveness, walkability, and the availability of facilities like parks, restaurants, stores, and cultural activities. The area's attractiveness and allure may have a significant impact on visitors' overall experience and happiness throughout their stay.

4. Local Zoning Ordinances and Regulations:

Check local zoning legislation and restrictions to ensure that the property is suitable for a bed and breakfast. Verify possible locations' zoning designations and understand any restrictions or regulations for land use, occupancy limits, parking, signs, noise, and other regulatory issues. Compliance with local legislation is critical for avoiding legal complications and maintaining the smooth operation of your B&B.

5. Property Characteristics:

Evaluate possible properties' size, layout, architectural style, and amenities. Consider if the property satisfies your operational requirements and provides the visitor experience you envisage. Consider the number of guest rooms, common areas, outdoor spaces, parking availability, and any extra features or services that may increase the appeal of your bed and breakfast to guests.

6. Competitive Landscape and Differentiation Opportunities:

Investigate the region's competitive environment to determine the presence of alternative lodging options such as hotels, vacation rentals, and other bed and breakfasts. Identify ways to set your B&B apart from the competition by providing unique facilities, customized services, themed experiences, or focused marketing methods. Understanding your competitive advantages will allow you to position your bed and breakfast properly in the market and attract customers.

7. Demand for Accommodation:

Determine the demand for lodging in the region based on visitor patterns, local events, seasonal fluctuations, and general market conditions. To determine the market potential for your bed and breakfast, consider occupancy rates, average daily prices, and guest preferences. Consider the existence of year-round demand or specialty markets, which may provide prospects for constant bookings and increased income.

8. Economic factors:

When evaluating suitable sites, consider economic issues such as property prices, taxes, insurance, and operational expenditures. Evaluate the financial viability of purchasing or leasing a property in the region, as well as its long-term investment potential. Consider the cost of renovating or upgrading the property to meet your desired standards, as well as any ongoing maintenance and utility fees.

9. Future Development Plans and Economic Trends:

Investigate future development plans, infrastructure projects, and economic trends in the region to predict prospective changes that may affect the value and appeal of the location for your B&B, Stay up-to-date on planned developments, redevelopment activities, and economic factors that may affect property values, tourism activity, and the general appeal of the area.

10. Personal preferences and lifestyle goals:

When deciding where to locate your bed and breakfast, keep your personal tastes, lifestyle objectives, and long-term intentions in mind. Choose a location that resonates with your business strategy and provides a quality of life that meets your requirements and preferences. When making your selection, consider proximity to your primary house, family commitments, community amenities, and lifestyle preferences.

Consideration on accessibility and facilities of the B&B location

When researching prospective locations for your bed and breakfast (B&B), you must c to provide a great guest experience and attract your target market.

Here's how to evaluate accessibility and amenities effectively:

Accessibility:

1. Transportation choices: Assess the location's accessibility by taking into account public transportation choices (bus, rail, metro), major roads, airports, and closeness to prominent tourist locations. Determine the ease of access to and from the B&B for visitors coming by car, airline, or other mode of transportation.

2. Proximity to Key Destinations: Evaluate the location's proximity to popular tourist attractions, cultural landmarks, outdoor recreational areas, dining options, shopping districts, and entertainment venues. Consider how easy it is for visitors to get to these destinations from your B&B and whether they can explore the region without traveling far.

3. Accessibility Features: Consider the property's accessibility features, such as wheelchair access, ramps, elevators, wide entrances, and accessible parking spots, to accommodate visitors with mobility issues or impairments. Ensure that the property meets accessibility requirements and regulations in order to create a comfortable and inclusive environment for all visitors.

Facilities:

1. Accommodation Facilities: Evaluate the property's facilities and amenities, such as guest room size, type (e.g., suites, cottages), and in-room amenities like private bathrooms, comfy beds, and quality linens. Consider if the accommodations are appropriate for your target market, which may include couples looking for romantic vacations, families with children, or business visitors.

2. Common Areas and Services: Evaluate the availability of communal spaces for guests to rest and mingle, such as a lounge, outdoor patio, garden, or dining area. Consider any additional services and amenities provided by the B&B, such as complimentary breakfast, afternoon tea, evening social hours, concierge services, spa treatments, recreational activities, or guided tours.

3. Recreational Facilities: Assess the availability of recreational facilities and amenities on the property or nearby, such as swimming pools, hot tubs, fitness centers, hiking trails, bike rentals, or water sports activities, to improve the guest experience and provide opportunities for leisure and relaxation.

4. Dining Options: Check whether there are on-site restaurants, cafés, or bistros nearby that provide breakfast, lunch, or supper to visitors. Examine the diversity and quality of the area's dining alternatives, which include local restaurants, cafés, food trucks, and specialist eateries catering to various tastes and preferences.

5. Additional Amenities: Consider any extra elements that might improve the visitor experience, such as complimentary Wi-Fi, parking, pet-friendly lodgings, bicycle rentals, laundry services, or business facilities (e.g., conference rooms, workstations).

When evaluating accessibility and facilities, you may select a site for your bed and breakfast that provides convenience, comfort, and a pleasant experience for your visitors. Consider your target market's demands and preferences, as well as the property's distinctive characteristics and surrounding location, to provide a great stay for your visitors and separate your B&B from competitors.

Navigating real estate and lease agreements

Navigating real estate and lease agreements is a critical part of starting a bed and breakfast (B&B) business. Whether you're buying a home or signing a lease agreement, careful consideration and negotiation are required to ensure a successful outcome.

Here's how to successfully navigate real estate and lease agreements:

1. Define your property requirements: such as location, size, layout, amenities, and budget. Consider accessibility, zoning regulations, and proximity to major attractions.

2. Conduct market research: learn about real estate market trends, property values, and rental rates in your desired location. Compare prices for comparable properties and determine the market demand for B&B accommodations in the area.

3. Hire a Real Estate Agent: Look for an agent or broker with experience in commercial or hospitality properties. An experienced agent can assist you with finding suitable properties, negotiating terms, and navigating the purchase or lease process.

4. Property Inspection: Conduct a thorough inspection of any property you're thinking about buying or renting. Examine the building, infrastructure, and amenities for potential problems or needed renovations.

5. Financial Considerations: Consider financing options for buying a home, such as mortgage loans, SBA loans, or private financing. Calculate the costs of acquiring the property, including the down payment, closing costs, property taxes, and ongoing expenses.

6. Negotiate Terms: Ensure the real estate transaction or lease agreement meets your needs and preferences. The purchase price, lease duration, rent amount, lease renewal options, maintenance responsibilities, and any allowances for property improvements are all potential negotiation points.

7. Conduct due diligence on the property: by reviewing zoning regulations, property records, title documents, environmental assessments, and any existing liens or encumbrances. Check the property's compliance with local regulations, and make sure there are no legal or financial issues that could jeopardize the transaction.

8. Legal Review: Ask a real estate attorney to review the purchase or lease agreement before signing. An attorney can assist you in understanding the terms and obligations, identifying potential risks or liabilities, and negotiating favorable terms on your behalf. When signing a lease agreement, it's important to carefully review the terms and conditions, such as rent escalation clauses, renewal options, maintenance responsibilities, property improvements, and restrictions on use or alterations.

10. Seek Professional Advice: Consult with real estate professionals, attorneys, accountants, or financial advisors who specialize in commercial and hospitality properties. Their expertise can be useful throughout the real estate transaction or lease negotiation process.

11. Finalize the Agreement: After negotiating and agreeing on all terms, sign and execute the purchase or lease agreement in accordance with legal requirements.

Navigating real estate and lease agreements necessitates extensive research, careful negotiation, and meticulous attention to detail. Understanding your needs, conducting due diligence, and seeking professional advice will help you navigate the process and secure a property that meets your requirements for starting and running a bed and breakfast business.

Designing and decorating your bed and breakfast (B&B)

Designing and decorating your bed and breakfast (B&B) is a fantastic opportunity to create a welcoming and comfortable space that reflects your individual style and improves the visitor experience.

Here are some important points to keep in mind:

Define Your B&B Style: Determine your B&B's general style and theme, such as comfortable and rustic, elegant and classic, modern and minimalist, or centered around a specific idea (for example, seaside escape, countryside charm). Select a unified design aesthetic that appeals to your target demographic and complements the property's architecture and surroundings.

Consider visitor comfort: When choosing furnishings and design, put visitor comfort first. Choose high-quality mattresses, sheets, pillows, and towels to ensure a restful night's sleep. Include comfortable resting places, reading nooks, and practical features like baggage racks, bedside tables, and enough storage space for visitors' possessions.

Design Inviting Plan welcoming common spaces where guests can rest, interact, and unwind. Consider adding comfy chairs, ambient lighting, and thoughtful extras like books, board games, and local artwork. Pay attention to the structure and flow of communal areas to encourage visitor interaction while also providing for seclusion and leisure.

Pay attention to specifics: Concentrate on the specifics to improve the overall visitor experience. Create a warm and friendly atmosphere by adding personal touches like fresh flowers, fragrant candles, and welcome items. Consider adding thoughtful services like complementary snacks, beverages, toiletries, and information about nearby sites and activities to improve visitors' stay.

Emphasize Cleanliness and Hygiene: Make cleanliness and hygiene a top priority in your bed and breakfast design and decor. Choose easy-to-clean surfaces, long-lasting materials, and washable textiles that can sustain heavy usage while remaining immaculate. Implement stringent cleaning methods and maintenance schedules to guarantee visitor safety and pleasure.

Incorporate Local Flavor: Incorporate parts of the local culture, tradition, and environment into your bed and breakfast decor and furniture. Showcase local artwork, crafts, and furnishings that reflect the destination's distinct personality. Provide locally produced facilities, goods, and experiences that emphasize the region's culinary pleasures, customs, and attractions.

Flexibility and Adaptability: When designing your B&B, keep flexibility and adaptability in mind to suit guests' changing requirements and preferences. Opt for adaptable furniture that can adjust to different group sizes, special events, or seasonal activities. Create multipurpose areas that can accommodate a variety of visitor preferences.

Consider implementing sustainable and eco-friendly design elements into your bed and breakfast, such as energy-efficient lighting, water-saving fixtures, and environmentally friendly materials. Choose furniture and décor created from renewable or recycled materials, and promote environmentally friendly activities across your business.

Seek Inspiration and Professional Advice: Learn about different design styles and trends by reading interior design periodicals, visiting websites, and using social media. Consider working with interior designers, decorators, or stylists that specialize in hospitality design to help bring your vision to life and create a unified and appealing atmosphere for your B&B.

Interior design trends

Interior design trends in the hotel business are always evolving to satisfy changing visitor preferences, improve guest experiences, and reflect modern design aesthetics. Here are some contemporary trends influencing interior design in hotels, resorts, and other hospitality establishments:

1. Biophilic Design: Biophilic design incorporates natural features and materials into interior spaces to enhance well-being and foster a connection with nature. This trend stresses the utilization of natural light, indoor plants, organic textures, and environmentally friendly materials to improve the visitor experience and provide a sense of calm and renewal.

2. Sustainable Design: Hospitality design is increasingly emphasizing eco-friendly techniques, energy efficiency, and responsible resource usage. Hotels and resorts are using sustainable materials, energy-efficient lighting and HVAC systems, water-saving fixtures, and renewable energy sources to reduce their environmental impact and attract environmentally concerned customers.

3. Flexible and Multifunctional Spaces: Hospitality facilities are increasingly adopting flexible and versatile rooms that can cater to a variety of visitor demands and activities. This trend incorporates flexible furniture arrangements, moveable walls, and adjustable layouts that allow spaces to smoothly shift between multiple uses, including dining, coworking, socializing, and events.

4. Technology Integration: Modern hospitality design prioritizes smart technology and digital advances to improve visitor convenience, comfort, and connectedness. This includes mobile check-in/out, keyless access systems, in-room automation, interactive digital displays, and high-speed Wi-Fi connectivity.

5. Hospitality Design: Incorporates locally sourced materials, artwork, and handmade aspects to celebrate local culture and workmanship. This trend celebrates regional identity, promotes local craftspeople and communities, and offers tourists an authentic and immersive experience that represents the destination's own character and customs.

6. A wellness-focused design: Promotes visitor well-being and holistic health by providing relaxing, rejuvenating, and thoughtful spaces. This trend includes amenities like specialized wellness areas (e.g., spas, exercise centers, meditation rooms), ergonomic furniture, circadian lighting systems, soundproofing, and air purification systems to improve visitor comfort and vitality.

7. Inclusive Design: This approach prioritizes accessibility, inclusion, and universal design principles to welcome visitors of all ages, abilities, and backgrounds. This trend includes elements like wheelchair-accessible facilities, barrier-free design, sensory-friendly settings, and amenities tailored to the different demands of visitors with disabilities or special needs.

8. Artificial Intelligence and Personalization: AI and data-driven technologies are being utilized in hospitality design to enhance the visitor experience and predict their preferences. This includes artificial intelligence-powered guest service robots, personalized digital concierge services, predictive analytics for room modification, and targeted marketing based on visitor behavior and preferences.

9. Hybrid Workspaces: With the rise of remote work and flexible schedules, hospitality facilities are adding hybrid offices to meet visitors' professional needs while traveling. This trend includes coworking spaces, business centers, and flexible workstations outfitted with high-speed internet, charging stations, ergonomic furniture, and multimedia conferencing capabilities.

10. Hospitality Design: seeks to create immersive and memorable experiences that engage the senses and elicit emotions. This trend incorporates experience features such as themed surroundings, interactive installations, immersive art installations, themed rooms, and storytelling components to fascinate and leave a lasting impact on guests. Shifting visitor expectations, technological improvements, sustainability concerns, and an increasing emphasis on guest well-being and individualized experiences fuel the changing world of hospitality design. Incorporating these trends into their design strategies allows hospitality facilities to create settings that delight visitors, identify their brand, and react to changing customer tastes in the dynamic hospitality business.

Sourcing furniture, décor, and amenities for your bed and breakfast (B&B)

Sourcing furniture, décor, and amenities for your bed and breakfast (B&B) involves considerable thought to ensure that you choose high-quality products that improve the guest experience while remaining within your budget and design style.

Here's how to properly source furniture, décor, and amenities for your bed and breakfast:

1. Define your style and budget: Before you start shopping for products for your bed and breakfast, decide on your design style and budget. Consider your desired overall look, such as rustic and comfortable, modern and minimalist, or classic and exquisite. Creating a clear budget will help guide your shopping selections and keep you within your financial limits.

2. Conduct research on suppliers and vendors: Conduct research to find reliable suppliers, dealers, and manufacturers of furniture, décor, and amenities who meet your quality and price expectations. Look for suppliers who specialize in hotel furnishings, have a proven track record of supplying high-quality items, and provide exceptional customer service.

3. Attend trade fairs and exhibits: To learn about new products, trends, and suppliers in the hospitality design and furnishings business. Trade exhibitions allow you to interact with vendors, see product samples, and negotiate prices and conditions directly with suppliers.

4. Online/Catalog Shopping: Investigate online platforms, catalogs, and websites that specialize in hospitality furniture, décor, and amenities. Many vendors provide online catalogs and shopping platforms where you may explore a large range of items, compare prices, and place orders directly from your computer or mobile device.

5. Visit furniture: Showrooms, retail stores, and design centers to evaluate product quality, comfort, and aesthetics. Showrooms allow you to try on furniture, compare finishes and textiles, and see how it will appear in your B&B.

6. Consider Customization Options: Customize furnishings, décor, and amenities to fit your design needs and branding. Many vendors provide customization services, which allow you to choose fabrics, finishes, and designs that complement your B&B's style and color palette.

7. Evaluate Quality and Durability: When choosing furnishings, décor, and amenities for your bed and breakfast, prioritize quality and durability. Choose high-quality materials that can survive repeated usage while maintaining their look over time. Look for furniture with a robust frame, long-lasting upholstery fabrics, and easy-to-clean and maintain finishes.

8. Eco-Friendly and Sustainable Options: When shopping for furnishings, décor, and amenities for your bed and breakfast, keep eco-friendliness and sustainability in mind. Look for things created from renewable resources, repurposed materials, or sustainably sourced wood. Choose energy-efficient appliances and fixtures to reduce your environmental impact and appeal to eco-conscious customers.

9. Negotiate pricing and terms: When buying things for your B&B, negotiate pricing and conditions with vendors to get the best bargains. Many suppliers provide discounts for large purchases, seasonal specials, or unique incentives to hospitality firms. Negotiate price, delivery dates, and warranty conditions to secure a fair arrangement for your B&B.

10. Testimonials and Reviews: Search for testimonials and evaluations from other hospitality firms or industry experts who have worked with the providers under consideration. Reading testimonials and reviews can provide useful information about product quality, customer service, and general satisfaction with the supplier's goods.

Chapter 5

Marketing and Branding

Marketing and branding are vital for starting and growing your bed and breakfast (B&B) business.

Branding

Creating a brand identity for your bed and breakfast (B&B) is a complex process that involves careful study and strategic preparation. Your brand identity is more than simply a logo or a name; it includes the values, personality, and distinctive offers that distinguish your B&B from rivals and appeal to your target audience.

Here are some strategies to consider:

- Begin by identifying your B&B's brand identity, including its USP, target market, values, and personality. Develop a memorable brand name and logo. Choose a memorable and unique name for your B&B that expresses its personality and ideals.
  Create a professional logo that graphically displays your business identity.

- Create a compelling website: Invest in a professionally created website that highlights your bed and breakfast's distinctive features, facilities, and guest experiences. Make sure your website is mobile-friendly and optimized for search engines. Use social media channels like Instagram, Facebook, and Pinterest to promote your B&B, communicate with customers, and post graphic material. Optimize your website and online listings for local SEO to boost visibility in search results.
- To remain in touch with former visitors and future customers, use email marketing to send newsletters, updates, and discounts on a regular basis. Create customized packages and promotions to increase reservations during off-peak seasons or holidays.
- Collaborate with local companies, attractions, and tour operators to provide special offers, packages, and suggestions to customers.

   Encourage pleased guests to post favorable reviews on platforms like TripAdvisor, Google, and Yelp.

- Create unforgettable experiences for visitors by hosting events, workshops, or themed weekends at your bed and breakfast.
- Engage with travel bloggers and influencers. Collaborate with travel bloggers, influencers, and social media celebrities to promote your B&B to their respective audiences.
- Continuously monitor and evaluate marketing performance with analytics tools and metrics. Implementing these marketing and branding techniques can help you successfully promote your bed and breakfast, attract customers, and establish a strong brand presence in the competitive hospitality business. To create a unified and memorable visitor experience, ensure that your brand message and values are consistent across all marketing platforms.

Concentrating on these key techniques and creating a brand identity that truly reflects your values, engages with your target audience, and provides outstanding guest experiences, can position your bed and breakfast as a trustworthy and memorable destination for visitors.

Marketing

Creating a detailed marketing plan is critical for efficiently marketing your bed and breakfast (B&B) and attracting guests. A well-thought-out marketing strategy will lay out your tactics for reaching your target demographic, increasing brand recognition, and driving bookings.

Here's a systematic strategy for designing your bed and breakfast's marketing plan:

1. Conduct rigorous market research to understand your target audience, competition, and industry trends. Determine the demographics, tastes, and habits of your ideal guests, as well as the distinguishing features of your B&B in comparison to rivals in your region.

2. Brand Positioning: Define your B&B's USP and market position. What distinguishes your B&B from others? Highlight the distinctive features, amenities, and experiences that will appeal to your target audience and set your B&B apart from the competition.

3. Segment your target audience by demographics, psychographics, and behavioral tendencies. Identify

multiple visitor personas and personalize your marketing messages and techniques to each segment's unique wants and interests.

4. Establish specific and quantifiable marketing objectives that correspond with your business goals. Whether you want to increase occupancy rates, increase direct bookings, or extend your visitor base, your marketing goals should be concise, attainable, and time-bound.

5. Develop marketing methods that efficiently reach your target audience. This might comprise a combination of online and offline approaches, such as: To increase exposure in internet searches, digital marketing involves optimizing websites for search engines (SEO). Use blog entries, articles, and guest tales to promote your B&B's unique features and experiences.

Use social media sites such as Instagram, Facebook, and Pinterest to communicate with your target audience, publish visual material, and promote special deals and events. Launch email marketing campaigns to nurture prospects, engage with previous visitors, and promote unique discounts and packages. Utilizing paid advertising on search engines

(Google Ads) and social media channels to target potential guests and boost direct reservations.

Offline marketing includes local advertising in travel periodicals, newspapers, and tourism brochures to attract potential visitors.

Networking and forming relationships with local businesses, tourist boards, and attractions in order to cross-promote their products and attract visitors. Participate in travel and tourist events, trade exhibits, and community festivals to promote your bed and breakfast and meet potential visitors in person.

6. Allocate your marketing budget among channels and methods based on their success in reaching your target audience and accomplishing goals. Consider the cost per acquisition (CPA), return on investment (ROI), and long-term viability of your marketing initiatives.

7. Create a clear implementation strategy that outlines activities, dates, and responsibilities for implementing marketing initiatives. Assign tasks to team members or external partners who will execute each technique, and keep track of progress on a regular basis to ensure deadlines are met.

8. Measurement and Analytics: To measure marketing success, establish KPIs and metrics. Monitor data like website traffic, conversion rates, social media engagement, and direct booking income to assess the performance of each marketing channel and change your tactics as needed.

9. Continuous Improvement: Evaluate marketing performance, identify areas for improvement, and adapt plans based on feedback and insights. Maintain a competitive advantage and create continuous development for your bed and breakfast by remaining nimble and sensitive to market changes, guest preferences, and industry trends.

10. Collect guest feedback through surveys, reviews, and direct conversation to better understand their experiences and preferences. Use this feedback to improve your marketing strategy, guest satisfaction, and the overall guest experience at your bed and breakfast.

When creating a marketing strategy for your bed and breakfast (B&B), it's critical to use a mix of online and offline marketing channels to successfully reach your target demographic and promote your establishment. Here's how to integrate both online and physical techniques into your marketing plan:

Online marketing channels

Site: Create a professional and user-friendly website for your B&B that highlights your lodgings, facilities, and distinguishing qualities. Optimize your website for search engines (SEO) to increase visibility in search results.

Social media: Use social media channels like Instagram, Facebook, and Pinterest to connect with potential visitors, provide visually attractive material, and promote special deals or packages. Interact with followers, answer comments, and utilize relevant hashtags to broaden your reach.

Email Marketing: Create an email list of previous visitors and future consumers, then send out frequent newsletters, updates, and specials. To boost interaction and reservations, personalize email messages based on visitor choices and interests.

Online Travel Agencies (OTAs): Partner with renowned OTAs like Booking.com, Airbnb, and Expedia to boost your B&B's online exposure and attract a larger audience. Optimize your OTA listings by providing intriguing descriptions, high-quality images, and competitive pricing.

Content Marketing: To attract and engage potential visitors, create useful and informative material on travel, local attractions, and guest experiences. Create a blog on your website, write guest posts on travel blogs, or make films highlighting your B&B and the local region.

Offline marketing channels:

Print Ads: Place advertisements in local newspapers, periodicals, and travel guides to market your bed and breakfast to locals and tourists visiting the region. Consider targeting media that appeal to your target group.

Brochure and Flyer: Create and distribute printed brochures and flyers highlighting your bed and breakfast's services, rooms, and special deals. Distribute these brochures to local visitor centers, tourist sites, and businesses that attract travelers.

Networking and Partnerships: Form ties with local companies, attractions, and tour operators to cross-promote one another's services. Collaborate with restaurants, vineyards, and event venues to provide unique packages or discounts to mutual clients.

Events and Open House: To attract guests and promote your B&B, host events, open houses, or themed weekends. Organize events like wine tastings, culinary courses, and live music performances to provide tourists with unforgettable experiences.

Direct Mailing: Send tailored direct mail marketing to potential guests in your target demographic, such as couples celebrating anniversaries or families booking holidays. Personalize your mailings and add appealing offers or discounts to promote reservations.

Combining online and offline marketing channels in your marketing strategy, you can successfully promote your bed and breakfast, attract customers, and boost reservations. Customize your marketing strategy for your target demographic, and continually assess and improve your efforts based on performance indicators and visitor comments.

Managing operations

Managing operations properly is critical to the success of your bed and breakfast (B&B) business. Efficient operations guarantee that your restaurant runs well on a daily basis, increases visitor pleasure, and contributes to its overall profitability.

Here's how to efficiently handle operations at your bed and breakfast:

1. Streamline booking and reservation processes: Create an effective booking and reservation system that allows customers to book online or by phone. Use booking management software to simplify the process, manage hotel availability, and track bookings efficiently.

2. Optimize Check-in and Check-out Procedures: Simplify procedures for a smooth visitor experience. To reduce wait times and increase visitor satisfaction, provide self-check-in, mobile check-in, and online check-in forms.

3. Effective Staff Management: Hire and educate competent employees committed to providing exceptional customer service. Clearly define roles and duties, develop standard operating procedures (SOPs), and offer continuing training and assistance to ensure that staff members are prepared to manage visitor queries and requests quickly.

4. Prioritize cleanliness and upkeep in order to maintain high levels of hygiene and appearance at your bed and breakfast establishment. To guarantee visitor pleasure and avoid bad reviews, implement regular cleaning schedules, conduct frequent inspections, and respond quickly to maintenance concerns.

5. Inventory and Supply Management: Maintain inventory and supplies, such as linens, toiletries, and amenities, to minimize shortages or overstocking. To meet guests' demands, set par levels for important commodities, evaluate inventory levels on a regular basis, and refill supplies on schedule.

6. Optimize housekeeping procedures to guarantee thorough and timely cleaning between guest visits. Create a systematic approach to housekeeping activities, offer essential cleaning equipment and supplies, and put in place quality control methods to ensure cleanliness.

7. Food and Beverage Management (If Applicable): Ensure effective food and beverage operations by obtaining fresh products, creating menus, and optimizing kitchen workflows. To keep expenses under control, train kitchen workers on food safety procedures, check inventory levels, and reduce food waste.

8. Utilize Technology and Automation: Use technology and automation tools to improve operations and efficiency. Use property management systems (PMS), channel managers, and online booking platforms to streamline administrative processes, manage bookings, and sync availability across several channels.

9. Monitor and analyze performance metrics: Monitor and evaluate important performance data on a regular basis, including occupancy rates, average daily rates (ADR), revenue per available room (RevPAR), and guest satisfaction scores. Use this data to find areas for improvement, make educated decisions, and optimize processes to get better outcomes.

10. Encourage visitor input through surveys, evaluations, and feedback forms to identify areas for improvement and

respond to complaints as quickly as possible. Use guest feedback to make improvements, improve guest experiences, and continuously improve your bed and breakfast operations.

Implementing these methods and concentrating on effective operations management can assure smooth day-to-day operations, increase client happiness, and drive the success of your bed and breakfast business. Continuously review and adjust your operations to meet evolving guest requirements and market realities, resulting in long-term success and profitability.

Recruiting and Training of Employee

When it comes to recruiting and training workers for your bed and breakfast (B&B), you must prioritize establishing a team that is not just experienced and knowledgeable but also embraces your establishment's values and hospitality standards.

Here's a full overview of how to handle hiring and training personnel for your bed and breakfast:

As an entrepreneur planning to create a bed and breakfast (B&B), one of the most important components of your business will be personnel selection and training. Your staff members will be the face of your B&B, interacting with visitors and ensuring that their stay is memorable and pleasurable.

Hiring Employees: When selecting personnel for your B&B, seek out people who not only have the essential skills and experience but also have a true love of hospitality and a kind personality. Consider conducting detailed interviews to analyze individuals' communication skills, customer service experience, and teamwork abilities.

Look for applicants who have a good work ethic, pay attention to detail, and have a positive attitude. Prioritize attributes like friendliness, professionalism, and a desire to go above and beyond to achieve customer pleasure. Keep in mind that personality qualities and attitude are sometimes just as essential as technical abilities while working in the hospitality industry. Offer an attractive salary and perks to attract excellent staff. Consider hiring people with a variety of talents and experiences to provide new views and expertise to your team.

Training Staff: Once you've recruited your team, it's critical to give them extensive training to guarantee they're prepared to provide outstanding service to your clients. Begin by familiarizing new employees with your B&B's policies, processes, and service standards.

Give hands-on training in areas including guest check-in and check-out processes, room cleaning and maintenance practices, and food and beverage service (where appropriate). Emphasize the significance of attention to detail, cleanliness, and professionalism in all aspects of their job. In addition, teach your personnel how to efficiently manage various visitor situations and questions, such as complaints, special requests, and offering local suggestions and information.

Encourage continual learning and development by allowing employees to attend training sessions, workshops, and industry events. Invest in their professional growth and skill development to ensure that they are always evolving and up to date on the latest trends and best practices in hospitality.

Create a friendly and supportive work atmosphere that promotes open communication, teamwork, and collaboration. Recognize and reward employees for their hard work and devotion, and foster an environment of mutual respect and admiration among team members.

Implementing Reservation Systems

To expedite your bed and breakfast's registration process, you must invest in a dependable reservation system that allows customers to reserve lodgings quickly and effectively. A reservation system allows you to manage hotel availability, track bookings, and interact with visitors more efficiently.

Here's how to establish a reservation system for your bed and breakfast:

1. Select the right reservation software: Research and invest in reservation software made exclusively for small accommodation enterprises, such as bed and breakfasts. Look for features like online booking, calendar management, guest communication tools, and reporting options.

2. Prepare Your Room Inventory: Enter your room inventory information into the reservation system, including room types, pricing, availability, and limitations (such as minimum stay requirements and blackout periods). To minimize overbooking, keep your room inventory accurate and up-to-date.

3. Configure booking options: Adjust the booking options in your reservation system to reflect your B&B's regulations and preferences. Set the minimum and maximum duration of stay, cancellation rules, deposit requirements, and any special deals or packages you provide.

4. Integrate with Online Channels: Integrate your reservation system with online booking channels such as your website, social media platforms, and third-party booking websites (for example, Booking.com or Airbnb). This allows customers to book directly through your website or other online channels, which improves ease and accessibility.

5. Train Staff for the Reservation System: Provide extensive training to your employees on how to utilize the reservation system properly. Make sure they understand how to use the system to handle bookings, process reservations, and interact with visitors. Regularly notify personnel of any system modifications or updates.

Check-In Procedures

Efficient check-in processes are critical for making a good first impression and offering a pleasant arrival experience for your visitors.

Here's how to develop excellent check-in processes for your bed and breakfast:

1. Pre-Arrival Communication: Before visitors arrive, give them a confirmation email or message with crucial information regarding their stay, such as check-in procedures, directions to your bed and breakfast, parking information, and any additional services or facilities offered.

2. Personalized Welcome: When guests arrive, greet them warmly and make them feel welcome. Provide a tailored welcome package or information sheet outlining your B&B, neighboring sights, food options, and any special events or activities taking place during their stay.

3. Efficient Check-in Procedure: Simplify the check-in procedure to reduce wait times and maximize efficiency. Prepare the essential papers in advance, including registration forms, payment processing, and any relevant identification or documents.

4. Room Orientation: Guide guests to their rooms and give them a quick overview of the room and facilities. Highlight major elements such as Wi-Fi access, temperature controls, the TV remote, and any other amenities or services accessible in the accommodation.

5. Guests Information: Gather any relevant guest information at check-in, such as contact information, special requests, and preferences. This information can be used to tailor the visitor experience and anticipate their needs during their stay.

6. Offer Assistance: Assist and guide guests as needed, such as making restaurant reservations, scheduling local excursions or activities, and recommending eating and touring alternatives in the region. Implementing effective reservation systems and check-in protocols can expedite the booking process and arrival experience for your visitors, guaranteeing a happy and memorable stay at your bed and breakfast.

Exceptional customer service

Delivering outstanding customer service is critical to the success of your bed and breakfast (B&B) business. Exceptional customer service goes beyond simply providing clients' fundamental requirements; it entails creating memorable experiences, anticipating their preferences, and going above and beyond to surpass their expectations.

Here's a full overview of how to provide outstanding customer service for your bed and breakfast:

As a bed and breakfast (B&B) entrepreneur, you should prioritize offering great client service. Exceptional customer service is more than simply satisfying customers' requirements; it's about providing unforgettable experiences that create a lasting impact and build guest loyalty.

Here's how you can deliver great customer service at your bed and breakfast:

1. Provide a warm and personalized greeting to guests upon their arrival. Personalize their experience by greeting them by name, providing a unique welcome message or gift, and inquiring about their preferences and requirements.

2. Anticipate Guest Wants: Know your visitors' wants and preferences before they ask. Pay attention to specifics stated throughout the booking process, such as dietary restrictions, special events, or specific requests, and handle them proactively to improve the visitor experience.

3. Responsive contact: Ensure open and responsive contact with visitors during their stay. Respond immediately to queries, requests, and comments, whether via phone, email, or in-person. Make visitors feel heard and respected by responding to their concerns and resolving any difficulties in a timely and professional manner.

4. Personalized service and attention to detail: To improve the visitor experience, provide individualized service and pay close attention to detail. Make personalized suggestions for local sights, eating alternatives, and activities based on your visitors' likes and preferences. Pay close attention to minor things like hotel amenities, turndown service, and extra touches that make visitors feel pampered and treasured.

5. Flexibility and Accommodation: Respond to visitors' needs and demands whenever feasible. Whether it's changing check-in/check-out timings, accommodating

dietary restrictions, or fulfilling specific requests, go above and beyond to meet and exceed guests' expectations.

6. Consistent Service Excellence: Ensure consistent service quality across your B&B, from housekeeping and maintenance to meal and beverage service (if applicable) and guest interactions. Ensure all employees are trained to consistently meet high service quality standards.

7. To provide great customer service, empower and assist your people with regular training, tools, and support. Encourage a culture of hospitality and collaboration in which employees feel respected, motivated, and empowered to surpass visitor expectations.

8. Proactive Problem-Solving: Address possible concerns or obstacles that visitors may have during their stay before they become problems. Be proactive in addressing guest complaints or difficulties, and take responsibility for resolving any issues that emerge to ensure visitors have a smooth and happy experience.

9. Solicit and Respond to Feedback: Actively collect visitor input through surveys, evaluations, and feedback forms, and utilize it to constantly enhance your bed and breakfast's

operations and service offerings. Take visitor input seriously and utilize it to create significant improvements and additions that are in line with their preferences and expectations.

10. Personalized Farewell: Express thanks for guests' stay and invite them to return in the future. Consider leaving a little parting gift or sign of thanks to make a lasting impression and promote recurring visits.

Maintaining a competitive

Maintaining a competitive advantage in the hospitality business, particularly in the bed and breakfast (B&B) sector, necessitates a strategic approach that emphasizes distinction, innovation, and continual development.

Here's a full explanation of how to keep a competitive edge Keeping a competitive edge for your bed and breakfast (B&B) is critical to attracting guests, generating money, and achieving long-term success as a hospitality entrepreneur. With increased market competition, it is critical to differentiate your bed and breakfast and strive for constant quality.

Here are some ways to keep your bed and breakfast competitive:

1. Differentiate Your Offering: Identify and emphasize unique selling features that distinguish your B&B from rivals. Whether it's your location, unique features, customized service, or themed rooms, highlight what makes your bed and breakfast unique and enticing to customers.

2. Prioritize visitor experience: Provide great service, customized touches, and unique experiences to ensure visitor happiness. Anticipate visitor requirements, surpass expectations, and go above and beyond to ensure each guest has a happy and memorable stay.

3. Embrace Technology and Innovation: Utilize technology to improve the passenger experience and streamline operations. Use property management systems (PMS), online booking platforms, mobile check-in/out choices, and other technology solutions to increase visitor efficiency and convenience.

4. Stay relevant to trends: Stay informed about industry trends, market insights, and guest preferences so that you can adjust and improve your products accordingly. Stay up-to-date on developing hospitality trends such as sustainable practices, wellness services, and experiential travel, and implement them into your B&B to remain relevant and enticing to visitors.

5. Promote sustainability and responsible tourism: Integrate sustainable and responsible tourist practices into your B&B operations. Implement eco-friendly activities, decrease waste, support local suppliers and craftspeople, and participate in community efforts to promote sustainability and attract eco-conscious visitors.

6. Invest in Marketing and Branding: Strategically promote your bed and breakfast to attract customers. Create a strong brand identity, use digital marketing platforms, work with influencers, and attend relevant events and promotions to increase your exposure and reach.

7. Develop a Positive Online Reputation: Manage and develop a positive internet reputation with guest reviews and testimonials. Encourage pleased visitors to submit good

ratings on review sites like TripAdvisor, Google, and Yelp, and respond quickly to any negative feedback or concerns to demonstrate your dedication to guest satisfaction.

8. Offer unique packages and promotions: Create unique packages, offers, and promotions to attract customers and encourage reservations, especially during off-peak seasons or holidays. Offer value-added packages, discounts for longer stays, or themed packages that cater to varied visitor tastes and interests.

9. Foster a culture of constant improvement and innovation in your bed and breakfast. Solicit input from guests and staff, examine performance indicators, and look for ways to improve and innovate in all elements of your business, from the guest experience to amenities and services.

10. Develop excellent ties with visitors, suppliers, local companies, and the community to foster support and collaboration. Collaborate with local attractions, tour operators, and restaurants to provide unique bargains or suggestions to clients, improving their entire experience.

Staying Current on Industry Trends

Keeping up with industry trends is critical to the success and growth of your bed and breakfast (B&B) business. The hospitality industry, which includes the bed and breakfast sector, is dynamic and ever-changing, with new trends emerging on a regular basis. Staying up-to-date on industry trends allows you to anticipate changes, adapt your strategies, and capitalize on opportunities to boost your B&B's competitiveness and guest appeal.

Here's a detailed discussion of how to stay up to date with industry trends for your bed and breakfast:

1. Research and Industry Publications: Stay up-to-date on industry trends by reading hospitality and travel-related publications, magazines, and websites on a regular basis. Subscribe to newsletters, blogs, and online forums where industry experts share their insights, analyses, and predictions for emerging trends.

2. Attend industry conferences and events: Participate in hospitality and tourism-related conferences, trade shows, and networking events. These events allow

attendees to learn about the most recent trends, innovations, and best practices from industry leaders, experts, and peers.

3. Networking and Collaboration: Develop a network of contacts in the hospitality industry, including B&B owners, hoteliers, suppliers, and industry professionals. Attend networking events, join industry associations or forums, and take part in collaborative projects to exchange ideas, share experiences, and stay current on industry trends.

4. Monitor guest feedback and reviews. Pay attention to guest feedback, reviews, and ratings on online platforms like TripAdvisor, Google, and social media. Analyze guest feedback and reviews to identify trends, preferences, and areas for improvement in your bed and breakfast operations, amenities, and services.

5. Stay up-to-date with technology. Stay up-to-date on technological advancements and innovations that affect the hospitality industry. Follow industry blogs, news websites, and technology forums to learn about new software solutions, mobile apps, and digital

tools that can help your bed and breakfast improve guest experiences, streamline operations, and increase its competitiveness.

6. Seek guidance and insights from hospitality industry experts, consultants, and advisors. Consult with professionals who specialize in marketing, revenue management, guest experience, and sustainability to gain valuable insights and stay current on industry trends and best practices.

7. Analyze market research and data. Use market research reports, surveys, and data analytics to learn about consumer behavior, market trends, and competitive dynamics in the hospitality industry. Analyze market trends, demographic shifts, and consumer preferences to identify areas for innovation and differentiation in your B&B.

8. Follow hospitality industry influencers, thought leaders, and B&B owners on social media platforms like LinkedIn, Twitter, and Instagram. Engage with their content, participate in discussions, and stay up-to-date on their insights, experiences, and

recommendations for industry trends and best practices.

9. Continuous Learning and Professional Development: Invest in ongoing education and professional development opportunities to stay current on industry trends and best practices. Attend workshops, webinars, and online courses hosted by industry associations, educational institutions, and professional organizations to expand your knowledge and skills in hospitality management, marketing, and operations.

10. Adapt and Experiment: Be willing to experiment and adapt to changing industry trends and guest preferences. Test new ideas, initiatives, and guest experiences in your B&B, collect feedback, and iterate on the results to stay ahead of the competition and meet your guests' changing needs. Staying informed and proactive about industry trends allows you to position your bed and breakfast business for success, anticipate changes, and capitalize on opportunities to improve guest satisfaction, drive

revenue growth, and maintain a competitive edge in the ever-changing hospitality industry.

Incorporating sustainable Practices

Incorporating sustainable practices into your bed and breakfast (B&B) operations is not only environmentally responsible, but it is also becoming increasingly popular among guests who prefer eco-friendly accommodations. By implementing sustainable practices, you can reduce your B&B's environmental impact, attract eco-conscious guests, and help to preserve natural resources.

Here's a detailed discussion of how to incorporate sustainable practices into your bed and breakfast:

As a hospitality entrepreneur, incorporating sustainable practices into your bed and breakfast (B&B) operations is critical for reducing your environmental impact, meeting guest expectations, and contributing to the global push for sustainability.

Here's how to integrate sustainable practices into your bed and breakfast:

1. Energy Efficiency: To reduce your bed and breakfast's energy consumption and carbon footprint, implement energy-efficient measures. Install energy-efficient appliances, LED lighting, and programmable thermostats to save energy. Encourage guests to save energy by turning off lights and electronics when not in use and adopting water-saving practices.
2. Water Conservation: Use water-saving measures to conserve resources and reduce usage in your B&B. Install low-flow faucets, showerheads, and toilets to reduce water waste. Encourage guests to reuse towels and linens during their stay to save water and energy for laundering.
3. Waste Reduction and Recycling: In your B&B, reduce waste generation and encourage recycling practices. Provide recycling bins in guest rooms and common areas so that guests can separate recyclable materials like paper, plastic, glass, and metal. Compost organic waste from the kitchen and dining areas.

4. Sustainable Food Practices: When possible, use locally sourced, organic, and seasonal ingredients in your B&B's breakfast offerings. Collaborate with local farmers, producers, and suppliers to promote sustainable agriculture and reduce carbon emissions from food transportation. Reduce food waste by carefully planning menus, effectively managing inventory, and donating excess food to local charities.
5. Provide eco-friendly amenities and supplies, such as biodegradable, recyclable, or sustainable materials. Provide toiletries in refillable dispensers rather than single-use plastic bottles. Use environmentally friendly cleaning products and supplies that are both non-toxic and biodegradable.
6. Green Building Practices: Integrate green building practices into your B&B's design and construction or retrofit existing facilities to improve energy efficiency and sustainability. Consider installing solar panels for renewable energy generation, using eco-friendly building materials, and improving building insulation to save energy.

7. Environmental Education and Awareness: Educate guests about your bed and breakfast's sustainable practices and encourage them to engage in environmentally friendly behaviors during their stay. Provide information and resources on local conservation initiatives, outdoor activities, and environmentally friendly attractions in the area.
8. Community Engagement and Partnerships: Form partnerships with environmental organizations, conservation groups, and sustainable tourism initiatives. Participate in community clean-ups, conservation projects, and eco-tourism activities to help the local environment and raise awareness about sustainability.
9. Certification and recognition: Obtain eco-certifications and accreditations for your B&B, such as Green Key, Earth-Check, or LEED certification, to show your commitment to sustainability and stand out in the market. Display prominently eco-friendly certifications and awards to highlight your bed and breakfast's environmental stewardship.

10. Continuous Improvement and Innovation: Continuously assess and improve your B&B's sustainability efforts by tracking energy and water consumption, waste generation, and environmental impact. Seek feedback from guests, staff, and stakeholders to identify areas for enhancement and innovation in your sustainability practices.

Seeking feedback

Seeking feedback and making constant improvements are critical components of running a successful bed and breakfast (B&B) business. You may improve the guest experience, operational efficiency, and business development by actively requesting input from guests, workers, and stakeholders and then using that feedback to make educated decisions and execute good changes.

As a hospitality entrepreneur, collecting feedback and always striving for improvement are critical to maintaining high standards, satisfying guest expectations, and driving the success of your bed and breakfast (B&B) business.

Here's how you can use feedback systems and promote a culture of continuous improvement in your bed and breakfast:

1. Guest Feedback: Collect feedback from visitors during their stay at your B&B. Give guests various ways to submit their thoughts, such as feedback questionnaires, online surveys, suggestion boxes, and direct connections with staff. Encourage guests to share honest feedback on their experiences, including what they liked and where they might improve.

2. Employee Feedback: Create a friendly atmosphere in which workers feel free to share comments and recommendations for improvement. Hold frequent meetings or one-on-one talks with employees to get feedback and ideas for improving operations, visitor happiness, and collaboration. Encourage open communication and constructive feedback among all team members.

3. Stakeholder Engagement: Collaborate with suppliers, partners, and local community members to obtain feedback and insights to improve your B&B's operations and decisions. Collaborate with stakeholders

to come up with ideas and projects that will help your bed and breakfast succeed and remain sustainable.

4. Evaluate feedback data: Collect and evaluate feedback from guests, staff, and stakeholders to find trends, patterns, and areas for improvement in your bed and breakfast operations, facilities, and services. Utilize qualitative and quantitative data analysis tools to acquire actionable insights and prioritize improvement initiatives.

5. Implement Changes and Solutions: Create action plans and strategies based on feedback and data analysis to enhance your bed and breakfast business. Implement modifications, solutions, and additions to visitor experiences, operational procedures, amenities, and facilities in response to guest input and to satisfy changing guest demands.

6. Measure and monitor success: Establish KPIs and measures to assess the impact of improvement projects on guest happiness, operational efficiency, and company success. To ensure continuous review and strategy modification, monitor KPIs on a regular basis and evaluate progress toward improvement targets.

7. Training and Development: Invest in training programs for B&B workers to improve their skills, knowledge, and service delivery. Provide regular training on areas such as customer service, communication skills, dispute resolution, and industry trends to help workers provide excellent guest experiences.

8. Innovative and Creative: Encourage innovation and creativity in your staff members by requesting ideas and proposals for new projects, services, and experiences that will set your B&B apart and please guests. Create a culture of innovation in which team members feel empowered to contribute to continual development.

9. Guest Follow-Up: After their stay, contact visitors to get comments and insights on their experience. Send out post-stay questionnaires or emails to get feedback on specific parts of their visit, such as rooms, facilities, and service quality. Use this feedback to identify areas for future development and demonstrate your commitment to guest happiness.

10. Celebrate Successes and Recognize Initiatives: Recognize and celebrate accomplishments from B&B improvement initiatives. Recognize and reward workers

that contribute to continuous improvement projects and provide great visitor experiences. Encourage a culture of acknowledgment and gratitude to drive further efforts toward excellence. By actively soliciting feedback, evaluating data, making adjustments, and cultivating a culture of continuous improvement, you can improve the guest experience, drive operational excellence, and position your bed and breakfast for long-term success and development.

Chapter 6

Financial management and revenue optimization

Financial management and revenue optimization are essential components of running a successful bed and breakfast (B&B) business. Effective financial management protects your B&B's financial health and longevity, while revenue optimization measures boost profitability and propel the firm forward.

Here's a thorough overview of financial management and income optimization for your bed and breakfast:

As a hospitality entrepreneur, good financial management and revenue optimization are vital to the profitability and sustainability of your bed and breakfast (B&B) firm.

Here's how you can handle your bed and breakfast's finances and maximize revenue:

Financial management

1. Budgeting and forecasting: Create a detailed budget that outlines your B&B's estimated income and costs in all areas of operation, including staffing, utilities, supplies, marketing, and maintenance. Assess and adjust your budget on a regular basis to reflect current performance and changing market conditions.

2. Expense Control and Cost Management: Choose cost-effective solutions that do not compromise service quality or visitor experience. Monitor your B&B's spending on a regular basis, find cost-cutting opportunities, negotiate better prices with suppliers, and streamline operational procedures to improve efficiency.

3. Effectively manage your bed and breakfast's cash flow to ensure there is adequate cash for everyday operations, investments, and unforeseen costs. Monitor incoming income and outgoing costs, maintain enough cash reserves, and use cash flow-improving tactics like early payment

discounts or payment policies to minimize outstanding receivables.

4. Financial Reports and Analysis: Generate and review financial reports on a regular basis to track your bed and breakfast's financial performance, analyze important indicators, and spot trends or opportunities for improvement. Use financial analysis tools and software to create accurate reports, examine profitability, and make data-driven decisions to enhance financial outcomes.

Revenue Optimization:

1. Pricing strategy: Create a targeted pricing plan for your bed and breakfast's accommodations and services to boost income while remaining competitive in the market. When deciding on hotel prices and additional services or packages, keep in mind seasonal demand, local events, rival pricing, and guest preferences.

2. Revenue Diversification: Think about growing your bed and breakfast's revenue streams beyond room bookings. Additional services and facilities, such as guided tours, culinary courses, spa treatments, or special events, can help

create extra income and attract customers searching for unique experiences.

3. Encourage direct bookings through your B&B's website or by phone to avoid third-party booking systems' commission costs. Encourage guests to book directly by providing unique discounts, loyalty awards, or value-added bundles. This will boost your bed and breakfast's profitability.

4. To increase revenue per visitor, use upselling and cross-selling techniques. Promote extra services, upgrades, or facilities during the booking process or during the visitor's stay. Train personnel to identify upselling opportunities and effectively explain the value proposition to guests.

5. Revenue management techniques: To optimize room rates and maximize income in the face of variable demand and market conditions, use dynamic pricing, demand forecasting, and yield management. Utilize revenue management software and tools to evaluate booking trends, dynamically modify prices, and maximize occupancy levels.

6. Utilize a CRM system to manage guest relationships, collect data, and tailor marketing to boost repeat bookings

and lifetime value. Use visitor data to segment your target demographic, customize marketing campaigns, and offer targeted specials or incentives to increase sales.

7. Improve the visitor experience by soliciting feedback through surveys, reviews, and direct communication. Use guest feedback to guide data-driven choices, fix any issues or complaints, and consistently enhance your bed and breakfast's offerings to increase visitor happiness and loyalty.

Pricing Strategies

Creating efficient pricing strategies for hotel rates and packages is critical to increasing revenue and profitability while keeping the market competitive. To maximize income and attract customers, pricing plans should take into account elements such as demand, seasonality, rival price, and guest preferences.

Here's a comprehensive overview of pricing options for room rates and packages for your bed and breakfast (B&B):

As a hospitality entrepreneur, creating effective pricing plans for room rates and packages is critical for increasing revenue and profitability in your bed and breakfast (B&B) business. Here's how you may use pricing techniques to maximize income and attract guests:

1. Dynamic Pricing: Use dynamic pricing tactics to alter hotel prices based on demand, seasonality, and market conditions. Use revenue management software and tools to evaluate booking trends, estimate demand, and dynamically alter prices to maximize revenue and occupancy levels.

2. Seasonal Pricing: Adjust hotel prices based on peak and off-peak seasons, local events, holidays, and other demand considerations. Adjust hotel prices higher during high-demand seasons, and offer discounts or specials during lull periods to encourage reservations and optimize income year-round.

3. Weekend vs. Weekday Pricing: Set different accommodation rates for weekends and weekdays based on demand and booking trends. Weekends and holidays usually fetch higher accommodation prices due to increased recreational travel, although weekdays may offer cheaper rates to attract business travelers and weekday customers.

4. Length of Stay Discounts: Provide discounts or incentives for guests planning longer stays, such as weekends, weeks, or monthly rentals. Implement tiered pricing systems to reward visitors with cheaper nightly prices for longer stays, promoting prolonged reservations and increasing occupancy.

5. Package Pricing: Offer value-added packages that include lodging, meal credits, spa treatments, guided tours, or unique experiences. Offer bundled packages at a lower cost than

buying individual components separately, creating extra value and encouraging customers to consider package offers.

6. Advance Purchase Discounts: Provide discounts or special prices for guests who book ahead of time. This encourages early bookings and helps estimate occupancy levels for your B&B. Implement tiered pricing, with escalating discounts for customers who book farther in advance, to encourage early reservations and maximize income possibilities.

7. Last-Minute Offers: Offer last-minute offers or flash sales for unsold merchandise near arrival dates to increase demand and fill remaining slots. Use targeted marketing efforts and promotional platforms to promote last-minute discounts and attract spontaneous visitors looking for lower rates.

8. Group Rates and Corporate Discounts: Provide reduced accommodation rates or customized packages for groups, corporate guests, and business travelers. Negotiate prices for corporate accounts, event groups, or wedding parties that reserve multiple rooms, cater to group travel needs, and increase occupancy during group events or business conferences.

9. Various rate alternatives: Offer various rate alternatives to accommodate diverse visitor preferences and booking patterns. Offer non-refundable, reduced prices for customers who are prepared to commit to their reservation in advance, as well as flexible, fully refundable pricing for visitors who want flexibility and peace of mind when making bookings.

10. Value-Based Pricing: Align room rates with your B&B's unique value proposition, focusing on excellent lodgings, customized service, and unique guest experiences. Communicate the value of your products effectively in order to justify higher fees and separate your B&B from the competition.

Overhead Management

Effective spending and overhead management are critical to your bed and breakfast's financial health and long-term viability. Controlling costs and expenses enables you to increase profitability, manage financial resources, and ensure long-term success. Here's a full discussion on controlling expenses and overheads for your bed and breakfast.

As a hospitality entrepreneur, you must efficiently manage costs and overheads to ensure the financial health and sustainability of your bed and breakfast (B&B) firm. Here's how you can manage expenses and overheads to save money and increase profits:

1. Budgeting and forecasting: Create a detailed budget outlining your bed and breakfast's predicted income and expenditure in all areas of operation, such as staffing, utilities, supplies, marketing, maintenance, and administrative costs. Use historical data, industry standards, and market trends to properly predict future expenditures.

2. Expense Control and Cost Management: Develop cost-effective techniques without sacrificing service quality or visitor experience. On a regular basis, monitor and track your B&B's spending, find areas for cost savings, negotiate better prices with suppliers, and streamline operational procedures to increase efficiency.

3. Personnel Optimization: Assess personnel requirements based on seasonal demand, occupancy, and business changes. Optimize staffing numbers to match task demands, eliminate overstaffing during slow periods, and use flexible scheduling strategies to save labor expenses while maintaining service standards.

4. Procurement and Inventory Management: Reduce expenses by streamlining procurement procedures and negotiating advantageous terms with vendors for supplies, linens, amenities, and other operational needs. Implement inventory management systems to monitor inventory levels, reduce waste, and avoid overstocking or stockouts, thereby improving inventory turnover and lowering carrying costs.

5. Energy Efficiency and Utilities Management: Implement energy-efficient techniques to minimize utility bills, including power, water, and heating and cooling prices. Upgrade to energy-efficient appliances, LED lights, and programmable thermostats to save energy and money on your utility costs. Monitor utility usage, identify areas for improvement, and put in place conservation measures to minimize consumption and expenses.

6. Maintenance and repair: Create a proactive maintenance plan to avoid expensive repairs and extend the life of your B&B's premises and equipment. Conduct frequent inspections, prioritize maintenance activities, and treat minor concerns as soon as possible to avoid costly future repairs or replacements. To save money, consider outsourcing maintenance services or forming relationships with reputable contractors.

7. Marketing and advertising: Align your marketing budget carefully to achieve the best return on investment (ROI) for your B&B's marketing and advertising. Choose cost-effective marketing platforms that efficiently reach your target audience, such as digital marketing, social media,

email marketing, and local partnerships. Monitor marketing performance indicators and adjust strategies needed to maximize ROI and reduce unnecessary costs.

8. Administrative and overhead expenditures: simplify administrative operations to decrease expenditures for office supplies, staff, software subscriptions, and other expenses. Consider cost-cutting techniques, including outsourcing administrative duties, using cloud-based software solutions, and obtaining bulk discounts for necessary services.

9. Insurance and Risk Management: Assess your B&B's in. Review insurance plans on a regular basis, compare quotations from several providers, and consider combining policies or changing coverage levels to reduce insurance costs while still providing enough protection against any liabilities.

10. Continuous Improvement and Monitoring:

Constantly monitor and review your B&B's costs and overheads in order to discover opportunities for improvement and adopt cost-cutting initiatives proactively. On a regular basis, review financial records, examine spending patterns, and compare your performance to that of industry peers to identify potential for cost savings and optimization.

Implementing efficient expense management measures and lowering overhead costs will help your bed and breakfast business improve its financial performance, profitability, and sustainability, resulting in long-term success and development in the competitive hospitality market.

Diversifying Revenue

Diversifying revenue streams is a good way to increase revenue, reduce risk, and ensure the financial viability of your bed and breakfast (B&B) business. Expanding beyond typical hotel reservations allows you to generate new revenue and improve the entire visitor experience.

Here's a full break about diversifying revenue streams for your bed and breakfast:

As a hospitality entrepreneur, diversifying income streams is critical for increasing revenue and guaranteeing the financial viability of your bed and breakfast (B&B) firm. Here's how you can diversify revenue streams to boost revenues and improve the client experience:

1. Additional Services and Facilities: Provide additional services and facilities to improve the visitor experience and create extra revenue. Consider offering guided tours, outdoor activities, culinary lessons, spa treatments, or wellness retreats based on your B&B's location and guest interests.

2. Food and beverage options: Increase the earning potential of your bed and breakfast by providing food and beverage options in addition to a complimentary breakfast. Consider offering lunch or supper to tourists, or create a café, restaurant, or bar on-site to attract both visitors and locals. Investigate food options for parties, weddings, and other special celebrations held at your B&B.

3. Special Events and Packages: Create customized event packages and promotions to entice visitors for holidays, festivities, and seasonal events. Offer themed packages, such as romantic getaways, gourmet weekends, or outdoor activity packages, to cater to varied visitor tastes and interests. To attract guests and generate additional revenue, host special events, workshops, or retreats at your bed and breakfast.

4. Retail and Merchandise Sales: Consider selling retail merchandise or branded products related to your bed and breakfast, such as toiletries, linens, apparel, or locally made artisan goods. Set up an on-site boutique or gift store to display and sell products to visitors as keepsakes or gifts, generating additional cash and promoting your B&B brand.

5. Venue Rental for Corporate Events: Use your B&B's facilities to host business meetings, retreats, workshops, or private events. Market your bed and breakfast as a one-of-a-kind, versatile event space that provides a charming and intimate setting for special occasions. To attract corporate clients and event organizers, provide venue leasing packages as well as event planning services.

6. Online Experiences and Workshops: Use digital platforms to provide virtual experiences, courses, or online classes that are relevant to your B&B's specialization or expertise. Organize virtual cooking courses, wine tastings, wellness sessions, or guided tours that customers can attend remotely, generating revenue from online reservations and virtual experiences.

7. Collaborations and Partnerships: Partner with local businesses, attractions, tour operators, or event organizers to create joint promotions, packages, or experiences that attract new customers. Partner with comparable businesses, such as spas, vineyards, outdoor adventure firms, or cultural destinations, to provide integrated packages and cross-promotion possibilities.

8. Membership and Loyalty Programs: To reward repeat customers and encourage loyalty, implement membership or loyalty programs. Provide members with exclusive benefits, discounts, or special perks, such as priority booking, complimentary upgrades, or access to member-only events and promotions, to encourage repeat bookings and increase customer retention.

9. Affiliate Marketing and Referral Programs: Investigate affiliate marketing opportunities and referral programs to increase revenue through collaborations with travel agencies, online booking platforms, and affiliate networks. Offer commissions or incentives for referrals that result in bookings at your bed and breakfast, thereby expanding your reach and attracting new guests via referral channels.

10. Integrate sustainable tourism initiatives and eco-tourism experiences into your B&B's values and environmental stewardship. Provide nature-based activities, wildlife tours, or outdoor excursions that promote responsible tourism practices and appeal to environmentally conscious travelers, generating revenue while also supporting conservation efforts.

Diversifying revenue streams and providing a variety of services, experiences, and amenities, you can increase income opportunities, attract a wider range of guests, and ensure your bed and breakfast's financial sustainability and success in the competitive hospitality industry.

Excellent Guest Experiences

Providing excellent guest experiences is critical to the profitability and reputation of your bed and breakfast (B&B) business. By may build loyal customers who return and promote your bed and breakfast by focusing on providing exceptional service, individual attention, and unforgettable moments.

As a hospitality entrepreneur, you must provide great guest experiences to ensure the success and reputation of your bed and breakfast (B&B) business.

Here's how to approach offering outstanding guest experiences at your bed and breakfast:

1. Individualized Service: Provide individualized service based on each guest's unique requirements and preferences. Take the time to learn about your visitors' tastes, dietary restrictions, special events, and any unique requests in order to tailor their experience and exceed their expectations.

2. Warm greeting and hospitality: When visitors arrive, greet them with a warm and genuine welcome, making a good first impression and establishing the tone for their stay.

Provide customized welcomes, such as welcome letters, welcome beverages, or modest welcome presents, to make guests feel cherished and loved.

3. Pay attention to detail in all aspects of the visitor experience, including room amenities, decor, eating, and leisure. Anticipate your visitors' needs, add thoughtful details, and make sure each interaction with your B&B exceeds their expectations.

4. Maintain perfect cleanliness and comfort in your B&B's amenities, including guest rooms, common areas, and outdoor spaces. Inspect and clean all areas on a regular basis, maintain comfortable bedding and furniture, and provide high-quality amenities to improve guests' comfort and happiness.

5. Provide interesting events and activities to improve guests' stays and create unforgettable memories. Organize guided tours, outdoor activities, culinary courses, wine tastings, or cultural events to highlight the local region and allow guests to engage and make memorable memories.

6. Exceptional Dining Experiences: Offer tasty, high-quality meals using locally sourced foods whenever feasible.

To guarantee that your B&B visitors have great dining experiences, offer a range of food selections, accommodate dietary needs, and give attentive service.

7. Prompt and Responsive Communication: Provide timely and responsive communication to visitors, from booking questions to post-stay follow-up. Respond immediately to visitor queries and requests, providing clear and thorough information, and offering help or advice to improve their experience and resolve any issues.

8. Personalized Recommendations and Concierge Services: Provide tailored advice and concierge services to help guests make the most of their stay and explore the surrounding region. Provide insider information on sites, restaurants, and activities; make bookings or organize transportation; and go above and beyond to meet visitors' needs and preferences.

9. Genuine Hospitality and Authenticity: Create a culture of true hospitality and sincerity among your employees that reflects your B&B's own personality and beliefs. Encourage employees to interact honestly with visitors, establish rapport, and make meaningful connections that leave a lasting impression and motivate guests to return.

10. Continuous input and improvement: Gather input from visitors via surveys, reviews, and direct communication to identify areas for improvement. Use guest feedback to make data-driven choices, respond quickly to any issues or complaints, and constantly improve your B&B's services to increase visitor happiness and loyalty.

In the competitive hospitality industry, you can differentiate your B&B by focusing on providing exceptional guest experiences that include personalized service, attention to detail, engaging activities, and genuine hospitality.

Here are two ways on how to approach a developing reservation systems and check-in procedures for your bed and breakfast.

- **Implementing reservation systems**

To expedite your bed and breakfast's registration process, you must invest in a dependable reservation system that allows customers to reserve lodgings quickly and effectively. A reservation system allows you to manage hotel availability, track bookings, and interact with visitors more efficiently.

Here's how to establish a reservation system for your bed and breakfast:

1. Select the right reservation software: Research and invest in reservation software made exclusively for small accommodation enterprises, such as bed and breakfasts. Look for features like online booking, calendar management, guest communication tools, and reporting options.

2. Prepare Your Room Inventory: Enter your room inventory information into the reservation system, including room types, pricing, availability, and limitations (such as minimum stay requirements and blackout periods). To minimize overbooking, keep your room inventory accurate and up-to-date.

3. Configure booking options: Adjust the booking options in your reservation system to reflect your B&B's regulations and preferences. Set the minimum and maximum duration of stay, cancellation rules, deposit requirements, and any special deals or packages you provide.

4. Integrate with Online Channels: Integrate your reservation system with online booking channels such as your website, social media platforms, and third-party booking websites (for example, Booking.com or Airbnb). This allows customers to book directly through your website or other online channels, which improves ease and accessibility.

5. Train Staff for the Reservation System: Provide extensive training to your employees on how to utilize the reservation system properly. Make sure they understand how to use the system to handle bookings, process reservations, and interact with visitors. Regularly notify personnel of any system modifications or updates.

- **Check-In Procedures**

Efficient check-in processes are critical for making a good first impression and offering a pleasant arrival experience for your visitors.

Here's how to develop excellent check-in processes for your bed and breakfast:

1. Pre-Arrival Communication: Before visitors arrive, give them a confirmation email or message with crucial information regarding their stay, such as check-in procedures, directions to your bed and breakfast, parking information, and any additional services or facilities offered.

2. Personalized Welcome: When guests arrive, greet them warmly and make them feel welcome. Provide a tailored welcome package or information sheet outlining your B&B, neighboring sights, food options, and any special events or activities taking place during their stay.

3. Efficient Check-in Procedure: Simplify the check-in procedure to reduce wait times and maximize efficiency. Prepare the essential papers in advance, including registration forms, payment processing, and any relevant identification or documents.

4. Room Orientation: Guide guests to their rooms and give them a quick overview of the room and facilities. Highlight major elements such as Wi-Fi access, temperature controls, the TV remote, and any other amenities or services accessible in the accommodation.

5. Guests' Information: Gather any relevant guest information at check-in, such as contact information, special requests, and preferences. This information can be used to tailor the visitor experience and anticipate their needs during their stay.

6. Offer Assistance: Assist and guide guests as needed, such as making restaurant reservations, scheduling local excursions or activities, and recommending eating and touring alternatives in the region.

Implementing effective reservation systems and check-in protocols can expedite the booking process and arrival experience for your visitors, guaranteeing a happy and memorable stay at your bed and breakfast.

Chapter 7

Keeping a competitive edge for your bed and breakfast

Keeping a competitive edge for your bed and breakfast (B&B) is critical to attracting guests, generating money, and achieving long-term success as a hospitality entrepreneur. With increased market competition, it is critical to differentiate your bed and breakfast and strive for constant quality.

Here are some ways to keep your bed and breakfast competitive:

1. Differentiate Your Offering: Identify and emphasize unique selling features that distinguish your B&B from rivals. Whether it's your location, unique features, customized service, or themed rooms, highlight what makes your bed and breakfast unique and enticing to customers.

2. Prioritize visitor experience: Provide great service, customized touches, and unique experiences to ensure visitor happiness. Anticipate visitor requirements, surpass expectations, and go above and beyond to ensure each guest has a happy and memorable stay.

3. Embrace Technology and Innovation: Utilize technology to improve the passenger experience and streamline operations. Use property management systems (PMS), online booking platforms, mobile check-in/out choices, and other technology solutions to increase visitor efficiency and convenience.

4. Stay relevant to trends: Stay informed about industry trends, market insights, and guest preferences so that you can adjust and improve your products accordingly. Stay up-to-date on developing hospitality trends such as sustainable practices, wellness services, and experiential travel, and implement them into your B&B to remain relevant and enticing to visitors.

5. Promote sustainability and responsible tourism: Integrate sustainable and responsible tourist practices into your B&B operations. Implement eco-friendly activities, decrease waste, support local suppliers and craftspeople, and participate in community efforts to promote sustainability and attract eco-conscious visitors.

6. Invest in Marketing and Branding: Strategically promote and brand your bed and breakfast to attract customers. Create a strong brand identity, use digital marketing platforms, work with influencers, and attend relevant events and promotions to increase your exposure and reach.

7. Develop a Positive Online Reputation: Manage and develop a positive internet reputation with guest reviews and testimonials. Encourage pleased visitors to submit good ratings on review sites like TripAdvisor, Google, and Yelp, and respond quickly to any negative feedback or concerns to demonstrate your dedication to guest satisfaction.

8. Offer unique packages and promotions: Create unique packages, offers, and promotions to attract customers and encourage reservations, especially during off-peak seasons or holidays. Offer value-added packages, discounts for longer stays, or themed packages that cater to varied visitor tastes and interests.

Create a culture of constant development and innovation inside your B&B. Solicit input from guests and staff, examine performance indicators, and look for ways to improve and innovate in all elements of your business, from the guest experience to amenities and services.

10. Develop excellent ties with visitors, suppliers, local companies, and the community to foster support and collaboration. Collaborate with local attractions, tour operators, and restaurants to provide unique bargains or suggestions to clients, improving their entire experience.

Sustainable practices in your bed and breakfast (B&B) operations

As a hospitality business, including sustainable practices in your bed and breakfast (B&B) operations is critical for reducing your environmental footprint, satisfying guest expectations, and contributing to the worldwide push for sustainability.

Here's how to implement sustainable practices in your bed and breakfast:

1. Energy Efficiency: Implement energy-efficient strategies to lower your bed and breakfast's energy use and carbon footprint. Install energy-efficient appliances, LED lights, and programmable thermostats to save electricity. Encourage visitors to save energy by turning off lights and devices when not in use and adopting water-saving practices.

2. Water Conservation: Use water-saving strategies to save resources and minimize use in your B&B. Install low-flow faucets, showerheads, and toilets to reduce water waste. Encourage visitors to reuse towels and linens during their stay to save water and energy for laundry.

3. Waste Reduction and Recycling: In your B&B, reduce trash creation and encourage recycling techniques. Provide recycling containers in guest rooms and communal spaces so that visitors may separate recyclable items, including paper, plastic, glass, and metal. Compost organic waste from the kitchen and eating areas.

4. Sustainable Food Practices: When feasible, include locally sourced, organic, and seasonal foods in your B&B's breakfast options. Collaborate with local farmers, producers, and suppliers to promote sustainable agriculture and minimize carbon emissions from food transportation. Reduce food waste by carefully planning menus, effectively controlling inventory, and donating extra food to local organizations.

5. Provide eco-friendly facilities and supplies, such as biodegradable, recyclable, or sustainable materials. Provide toiletries in refillable dispensers rather than single-use disposable bottles. Use environmentally friendly cleaning solutions and supplies that are both non-toxic and biodegradable.

6. Green Building Principles: Integrate green building principles into your B&B's design and construction, or remodel existing buildings to increase energy efficiency and sustainability. Consider adding solar panels for sustainable energy generation, employing eco-friendly building materials, and improving building insulation to save energy.

7. Environmental Education and Awareness: Educate visitors about your bed and breakfast's sustainable operations and urge them to engage in environmentally responsible habits throughout their stay. Provide information and resources on local conservation projects, outdoor activities, and environmentally friendly attractions in the region.

8. Community Engagement and Collaborations: Form collaborations with environmental organizations, conservation groups, and sustainable tourism projects. Participate in community clean-ups, conservation initiatives, and eco-tourism activities to help the local environment and increase awareness about sustainability.

9. Certification and recognition: Obtain eco-certifications and accreditations for your B&B, such as Green Key, Earth Check, or LEED certification, to show your dedication to sustainability and stand out in the market. Display eco-friendly certificates and accolades in public to highlight your bed and breakfast's environmental responsibility.

10. Continuous Improvement and Innovation: Continuously assess and improve your B&B's sustainability efforts by tracking energy and water use, trash creation, and environmental effects. Seek input from visitors, workers, and stakeholders to discover opportunities for enhancement and innovation in your sustainable operations.

Gathering of Feed Back for Improvement

As a hospitality entrepreneur, collecting feedback and always striving for improvement are critical to maintaining high standards, satisfying guest expectations, and driving the success of your bed and breakfast (B&B) business.

Here's how you can use feedback systems and promote a culture of continuous improvement in your bed and breakfast:

1. Guest Feedback: Collect feedback from visitors during their stay at your B&B. Give guests various ways to submit their thoughts, such as feedback questionnaires, online surveys, suggestion boxes, and direct connections with staff. Encourage guests to share honest feedback on their experiences, including what they liked and where they might improve.

2. Employee Feedback: Create a friendly atmosphere in which workers feel free to share comments and recommendations for improvement. Hold frequent meetings or one-on-one talks with employees to get feedback and ideas for improving operations, visitor happiness, and collaboration. Encourage open communication and constructive feedback among all team members.

3. Stakeholder Engagement: Collaborate with suppliers, partners, and local community members to obtain feedback and insights to improve your B&B's operations and decisions. Collaborate with stakeholders to come up with ideas and projects that will help your bed and breakfast succeed and remain sustainable.

4. Evaluate feedback data: Collect and evaluate feedback from guests, staff, and stakeholders to find trends, patterns, and areas for improvement in your bed and breakfast operations, facilities, and services. Utilize qualitative and quantitative data analysis tools to acquire actionable insights and prioritize improvement initiatives.

5. Implement Changes and Solutions: Create action plans and strategies based on feedback and data analysis. Implement modifications, solutions, and additions to visitor experiences, operational procedures, amenities, and facilities in response to guest input and to satisfy changing guest demands.

6. Measure and monitor success: Establish KPIs and measures to assess the impact of improvement projects on guest happiness, operational efficiency, and company success. To ensure continuous review and strategy modification, monitor KPIs on a regular basis and evaluate progress toward improvement targets.

7. Training and Development: Invest in training programs for B&B workers to improve their skills, knowledge, and service delivery. Provide regular training on areas such as customer service, communication skills, dispute resolution, and industry trends to help workers provide excellent guest experiences.

8. Innovative and Creative: Encourage innovation and creativity in your staff members by requesting ideas and proposals for new projects, services, and experiences that will set your B&B apart and please guests. Create a culture of innovation in which team members feel empowered to contribute to continual development.

9. Guest Follow-Up: After their stay, contact visitors to get comments and insights on their experience. Send out post-stay questionnaires or emails to get feedback on specific parts of their visit, such as rooms, facilities, and service quality. Use this feedback to identify areas for future development and demonstrate your commitment to guest happiness.

10. Celebrate Successes and Recognize Initiatives: Recognize and celebrate accomplishments from B&B improvement initiatives. Recognize and reward workers that contribute to continuous improvement projects and provide great visitor experiences. Encourage a culture of acknowledgment and gratitude to drive further efforts toward excellence.

CHAPTER 8

Financial Management and Revenue Optimization

Financial management and revenue optimization are key components of running a profitable bed and breakfast (B&B) business. Effective financial management assures your B&B's financial health and sustainability, while revenue optimization tactics increase profitability and promote company development.

As a hospitality entrepreneur, good financial management and revenue optimization are critical to your bed and breakfast (B&B) firm's profitability and sustainability.

Here's how you might handle financial management and revenue optimization for your bed and breakfast:

Financial Management

1. Budgeting and forecasting: Create a thorough budget outlining your B&B's predicted income and costs in all areas of operation, such as staffing, utilities, supplies, marketing, and maintenance. Regularly assess and revise your budget to reflect actual performance and changing market circumstances.

2. Expense Control and Cost Management: Implement cost-effective techniques without sacrificing service quality or visitor experience. On a regular basis, monitor and track your B&B's spending, find areas for cost savings, negotiate better prices with suppliers, and streamline operational procedures to increase efficiency.

3. Effectively manage your bed and breakfast's cash flow to guarantee enough liquidity for daily operations, investments, and unexpected costs. Monitor incoming income and outgoing costs, keep enough cash reserves, and adopt cash flow-improving tactics such as early payment discounts or payment policies to minimize outstanding receivables.

4. Financial Reporting and Analysis: Generate and review financial reports on a regular basis to monitor your bed and breakfast's financial performance, examine important indicators, and spot trends or areas for development. Use financial analysis tools and software to create accurate reports, examine profitability, and make data-driven decisions to improve financial results.

Revenue Optimization

1. Pricing strategy: Create a targeted pricing plan for your B&B's accommodations and services to increase income while remaining competitive in the market. Consider seasonal demand, local events, rival pricing, and guest preferences when determining hotel rates and pricing for extra services or packages.

2. Revenue Diversification: Consider expanding your B&B's revenue streams beyond room bookings. To earn extra income and attract customers looking for unique experiences, provide additional services and facilities such as guided tours, culinary lessons, spa treatments, or special events.

3. Promote direct bookings through your B&B's website or phone reservations to reduce commission costs from third-party booking systems. Incentivize visitors to book directly by offering unique discounts, loyalty awards, or value-added packages. This will boost your B&B's profitability.

4. Implement upselling and cross-selling strategies to increase guest income. Promote extra services, upgrades, or amenities during the booking or guest stay. Train employees to recognize upsell opportunities and effectively explain the value offer to guests.

5. Income Management Techniques: Use dynamic pricing, demand forecasting, and yield management to optimize room rates and maximize income throughout variable demand and market circumstances. Use revenue management software and tools to evaluate booking trends, alter prices dynamically, and maximize occupancy levels.

6. Implement a CRM system to manage guest connections, gather data, and customize marketing to enhance repeat bookings and lifetime value. Use guest data to segment your target demographic, adapt marketing campaigns, and provide targeted specials or incentives to boost sales.

7. Ask guests for feedback using surveys, reviews, and direct conversation in order to improve the guest experience. Use guest feedback to inform data-driven choices, fix any issues or concerns, and constantly enhance your B&B's offerings to boost visitor happiness and loyalty.

Implementing effective financial management practices and revenue optimization strategies can help your bed and breakfast business improve its financial performance, profitability, and sustainability, ultimately driving long-term success and growth in the competitive hospitality industry.

CREATING EFFICIENT PRICING STRATEGIES

Creating efficient pricing strategies for hotel rates and packages is critical to increasing revenue and profitability while keeping the market competitive. To maximize income and attract customers, pricing plans should take into account elements such as demand, seasonality, rival price, and guest preferences.

Here's a comprehensive overview of pricing options for room rates and packages for your bed and breakfast (B&B):

1. Dynamic Pricing: Use dynamic pricing tactics to alter hotel prices based on demand, seasonality, and market conditions. Use revenue management software and tools to evaluate booking trends, estimate demand, and dynamically alter prices to maximize revenue and occupancy levels.

2. Seasonal Pricing: Adjust hotel prices based on peak and off-peak seasons, local events, holidays, and other demand considerations. Adjust hotel prices higher during high-demand seasons, and offer discounts or specials during lull periods to encourage reservations and optimize income year-round.

3. Weekend vs. Weekday Pricing: Set different accommodation rates for weekends and weekdays based on demand and booking trends. Weekends and holidays usually fetch higher accommodation prices due to increased recreational travel, although weekdays may offer cheaper rates to attract business travelers and weekday customers.

4. Length of Stay Discounts: Provide discounts or incentives for guests planning longer stays, such as weekends, weeks, or monthly rentals. Implement tiered pricing systems to reward visitors with cheaper nightly prices for longer stays, promoting prolonged reservations and increasing occupancy.

5. Package Pricing: Offer value-added packages that include lodging, meal credits, spa treatments, guided tours, or unique experiences. Offer bundled packages at a lower cost than buying individual components separately, creating extra value and encouraging customers to consider package offers.

6. Advance Purchase Discounts: Provide discounts or special prices for guests who book ahead of time. This encourages early bookings and helps estimate occupancy levels for your B&B. Implement tiered pricing, with escalating discounts for customers who book farther in advance, to encourage early reservations and maximize income possibilities.

7. Last-Minute Offers: Offer last-minute offers or flash sales for unsold merchandise near arrival dates to increase demand and fill remaining slots. Use targeted marketing efforts and promotional platforms to promote last-minute discounts and attract spontaneous visitors looking for lower rates.

8. Group Rates and Corporate Discounts: Provide reduced accommodation rates or customized packages for groups, corporate guests, and business travelers. Negotiate prices for corporate accounts, event groups, or wedding parties that reserve multiple rooms, cater to group travel needs, and increase occupancy during group events or business conferences.

9. Various rate alternatives: Offer various rate alternatives to accommodate diverse visitor preferences and booking patterns. Offer non-refundable, reduced prices for customers who are prepared to commit to their reservation in advance, as well as flexible, fully refundable pricing for visitors who want flexibility and peace of mind when making bookings.

10. Value-Based Pricing: Align room rates with your B&B's unique value proposition, focusing on excellent lodgings, customized service, and unique guest experiences. Communicate the value of your products effectively in order to justify higher fees and separate your B&B from the competition.

Employing smart pricing strategies for room rates and packages, you can increase revenue, maximize occupancy, and attract guests to your bed and breakfast while remaining competitive and profitable in the ever-changing hospitality sector.

Effective Spending and Overhead Management

Effective spending and overhead management are critical to your bed and breakfast's financial health and long-term viability. Controlling costs and expenses enables you to increase profitability, manage financial resources, and ensure long-term success.

Here's a full discussion on controlling expenses and overheads for your bed and breakfast.

1. Budgeting and forecasting: Create a detailed budget outlining your bed and breakfast's predicted income and expenditure in all areas of operation, such as staffing, utilities, supplies, marketing, maintenance, and administrative costs. Use historical data, industry standards, and market trends to properly predict future expenditures.

2. Expense Control and Cost Management: Develop cost-effective techniques without sacrificing service quality or visitor experience. On a regular basis, monitor and track your B&B's spending, find areas for cost savings, negotiate better prices with suppliers, and streamline operational procedures to increase efficiency.

3. Personnel Optimization: Assess personnel requirements based on seasonal demand, occupancy, and business changes. Optimize staffing numbers to match task demands, eliminate overstaffing during slow periods, and use flexible scheduling strategies to save labor expenses while maintaining service standards.

4. Procurement and Inventory Management: Reduce expenses by streamlining procurement procedures and negotiating advantageous terms with vendors for supplies, linens, amenities, and other operational needs. Implement inventory management systems to monitor inventory levels, reduce waste, and avoid overstocking or stockouts, thereby improving inventory turnover and lowering carrying costs.

5. Energy Efficiency and Utilities Management: Implement energy-efficient techniques to minimize utility bills, including power, water, and heating and cooling prices. Upgrade to energy-efficient appliances, LED lights, and programmable thermostats to save energy and money on your utility costs. Monitor utility usage, identify areas for improvement, and put in place conservation measures to minimize consumption and expenses.

6. Maintenance and repair: Create a proactive maintenance plan to avoid expensive repairs and extend the life of your B&B's premises and equipment. Conduct frequent inspections, prioritize maintenance activities, and treat minor concerns as soon as possible to avoid costly future repairs or replacements. To save money, consider outsourcing maintenance services or forming relationships with reputable contractors.

7. Marketing and advertising: Align your marketing budget carefully to achieve the best return on investment (ROI) for your B&B's marketing and advertising. Choose cost-effective marketing platforms that efficiently reach your target audience, such as digital marketing, social media, email marketing, and local partnerships. Monitor marketing performance indicators and adjust strategies as needed to maximize ROI and reduce unnecessary costs.

8. Administrative and overhead expenditures: simplify administrative operations to decrease expenditures for office supplies, staff, software subscriptions, and other expenses. Consider cost-cutting techniques, including outsourcing administrative duties, using cloud-based software solutions, and obtaining bulk discounts for necessary services.

9. Insurance and Risk Management: Assess your B&B's insurance coverage and risk management procedures. Review insurance plans on a regular basis, compare quotations from several providers, and consider combining policies or changing coverage levels to reduce insurance costs while still providing enough protection against any liabilities.

10. Continuous Improvement and Monitoring: Constantly monitor and review your B&B's costs and overheads in order to discover opportunities for improvement and adopt cost-cutting initiatives proactively. On a regular basis, review financial records, examine spending patterns, and compare your performance to that of industry peers to identify potential for cost savings and optimization.

Implementing efficient expense management measures and lowering overhead costs will help your bed and breakfast business improve its financial performance, profitability, and sustainability, resulting in long-term success and development in the competitive hospitality market.

Diversifying Revenue Streams

Diversifying revenue streams is a good way to increase revenue, reduce risk, and ensure the financial viability of your bed and breakfast (B&B) business. Expanding beyond typical hotel reservations allows you to generate new revenue and improve the entire visitor experience.

Here's a full talk about diversifying revenue streams for your bed and breakfast:

1. Additional Services and Facilities: Provide additional services and facilities to improve the visitor experience and create extra revenue. Consider offering guided tours, outdoor activities, culinary lessons, spa treatments, or wellness retreats based on your B&B's location and guest interests.

2. Food and beverage options: Increase the earning potential of your bed and breakfast by providing food and beverage options in addition to a complimentary breakfast. Consider offering lunch or supper to tourists, or create a café, restaurant, or bar on-site to attract both visitors and locals. Investigate food options for parties, weddings, and other special celebrations held at your B&B.

3. Special Events and Packages: Create customized event packages and promotions to entice visitors for holidays, festivities, and seasonal events. Offer themed packages, such as romantic getaways, gourmet weekends, or outdoor activity packages, to cater to varied visitor tastes and interests. To attract guests and generate additional revenue, host special events, workshops, or retreats at your bed and breakfast.

4. Retail and Merchandise Sales: Consider offering retail merchandise or branded products relevant to your bed and breakfast, such as toiletries, bedding, clothes, or locally made artisan goods. Set up an on-site boutique or gift store to display and sell products to visitors as keepsakes or gifts, generating additional cash and promoting your B&B brand.

5. Venue Rental for Corporate Events: Use your B&B's facilities to host business meetings, retreats, workshops, or private events. Market your bed and breakfast as a one-of-a-kind, multipurpose event venue that provides a pleasant and private atmosphere for special events. To attract corporate clients and event organizers, provide venue leasing packages as well as event planning services.

6. Online Experiences and Workshops: Use digital platforms to provide virtual experiences, courses, or online classes that are relevant to your B&B's specialization or expertise. Organize virtual cooking courses, wine tastings, wellness sessions, or guided tours that customers can attend remotely, generating revenue from online reservations and virtual experiences.

7. Collaborations and Partnerships: Partner with local companies, attractions, tour operators, or event organizers to develop combined promotions, packages, or experiences that attract new customers. Partner with comparable businesses, such as spas, vineyards, outdoor adventure firms, or cultural destinations, to provide integrated packages and cross-promotion possibilities.

8. Membership and Loyalty Programs: To reward repeat customers and encourage loyalty, implement membership or loyalty programs. Provide members with unique privileges, discounts, or special perks, such as priority booking, gratis upgrades, or access to member-only events and promotions, to encourage repeat reservations and increase customer retention.

9. Affiliate Marketing and Referral Programs: Investigate affiliate marketing options and referral programs to increase income through collaborations with travel agents, internet booking platforms, and affiliate networks. Offer rewards or incentives for recommendations that result in bookings at your bed and breakfast, increasing your reach and attracting new customers via referral networks.

10. Integrate sustainable tourism projects and eco-tourism experiences. Provide nature-based activities, animal tours, or outdoor excursions that encourage responsible tourism practices and appeal to environmentally concerned visitors, making cash while also supporting conservation initiatives.

Providing Excellent Guest Experiences

Providing excellent guest experiences is critical to the profitability and reputation of your bed and breakfast (B&B) business. By may build loyal customers who return and promote your bed and breakfast by focusing on providing exceptional service, individual attention, and unforgettable moments.

Here's a full overview of how to deliver outstanding guest experiences at your bed and breakfast:

1. Individualized Service: Provide individualized service based on each guest's unique requirements and preferences. Take the time to learn about your visitors' tastes, dietary restrictions, special events, and any unique requests in order to tailor their experience and exceed their expectations.

2. Warm greeting and hospitality: When visitors arrive, greet them with a warm and genuine welcome, making a good first impression and establishing the tone for their stay. Provide customized welcomes, such as welcome letters, welcome beverages, or modest welcome presents, to make guests feel cherished and loved.

3. Pay attention to detail in all aspects of the visitor experience, including room amenities, decor, eating, and leisure. Anticipate your visitors' needs, add thoughtful details, and make sure each interaction with your B&B exceeds their expectations.

4. Maintain perfect cleanliness and comfort in your B&B's amenities, including guest rooms, common areas, and outdoor spaces. Inspect and clean all areas on a regular basis, maintain comfortable bedding and furniture, and provide high-quality amenities to improve guests' comfort and happiness.

5. Provide interesting events and activities to improve guests' stays and create unforgettable memories. Organize guided tours, outdoor activities, culinary courses, wine tastings, or

cultural events to highlight the local region and allow guests to engage and make memorable memories.

6. Exceptional Dining Experiences: Offer tasty, high-quality meals using locally sourced foods whenever feasible. To guarantee that your B&B visitors have great dining experiences, offer a range of food selections, accommodate dietary needs, and give attentive service.

7. Prompt and Responsive Communication: Provide timely and responsive communication to visitors, from booking questions to post-stay follow-up. Respond immediately to visitor queries and requests, providing clear and thorough information, and offering help or advice to improve their experience and resolve any issues.

8. Personalized Recommendations and Concierge Services: Provide tailored advice and concierge services to help guests make the most of their stay and explore the surrounding region. Provide insider information on sites, restaurants, and activities; make bookings or organize transportation; and go above and beyond to meet visitors' needs and preferences.

9. Genuine Hospitality and Authenticity: Create a culture of true hospitality and sincerity among your employees that reflects your B&B's own personality and beliefs. Encourage employees to interact honestly with visitors, establish rapport, and make meaningful connections that leave a lasting impression and motivate guests to return.

10. Continuous input and improvement: Gather input from visitors via surveys, reviews, and direct communication to identify areas for improvement. Use guest feedback to make data-driven choices, respond quickly to any issues or complaints, and constantly improve your B&B's services to increase visitor happiness and loyalty.

In the competitive hospitality industry, you can differentiate your B&B by focusing on providing exceptional guest experiences that include personalized service, attention to detail, engaging activities, and genuine hospitality.

Personalizing Services and Facilities

Personalizing services and facilities is an important method for improving the visitor experience and generating memorable stays at a bed and breakfast (B&B). Understanding customers' preferences and anticipating their requirements allows you to adjust your services and provide a unique and personalized experience that surpasses their expectations.

Here's a full explanation of how to tailor services and facilities at your bed and breakfast.

1. Pre-Arrival Communication: Communicate with visitors before they arrive to learn about their preferences, special requests, and any requirements they may have during their stay. Send individualized pre-arrival emails or surveys to collect important information and adapt the experience accordingly.

2. Customized Room Setup: Customize the room layout and facilities to suit visitors' tastes and special events. Provide alternatives for room layouts (e.g., king-size bed vs. twin beds), pillow preferences, additional blankets or pillows, and unique extras like welcome baskets, fresh flowers, or customized messages.

3. Dietary Preferences and Restrictions: Catering to customers' dietary choices and constraints, provide customizable breakfast alternatives that fit diverse dietary demands, such as vegetarian, vegan, gluten-free, or allergy-friendly meals. Take notice of visitors' dietary limitations during the booking process and adapt food offerings accordingly.

4. Personalized Concierge Services: Help customers plan their schedule, make meal reservations, arrange transportation, and organize special excursions and experiences. Provide insider information, local suggestions, and tailored support to help them enjoy their stay and create unforgettable experiences.

5. Memorable Occasion Celebrations: Celebrate memorable occasions like birthdays, anniversaries, or milestones with visitors staying at your B&B. Provide complimentary enhancements, extra luxuries, or personalized surprises to make their celebration unforgettable and leave a lasting impression.

6. Tailored Experiences and Activities: Customize experiences and activities based on visitors' interests and preferences. Offer guided tours, outdoor adventures, gourmet experiences, wellness activities, and cultural excursions to meet the needs of a diverse range of guests.

7. Individualized Amenities and Services: Offer individualized amenities and services to meet customers' unique requirements and preferences. Provide in-room massage treatments, turndown service with bespoke snacks or beverages, and tailored minibar selections depending on guest preferences.

8. Recognize and reward repeat visitors for their commitment by providing tailored incentives, discounts, or special luxuries throughout their stay. Recognize their previous visits and make their current stay even more memorable to show your thanks for their continuous support and commitment to your bed and breakfast.

9. Feedback and Follow-Up: Collect feedback from visitors throughout their stay and follow up with them after departure to learn about their experience and identify areas for improvement. Use visitor feedback to constantly improve your B&B's offerings and tailor future guest experiences to their preferences and ideas.

10. Predict visitors' wants and preferences based on their profile, past encounters, and expressed preferences. Proactively address any possible issues or complaints, provide personalized recommendations, and go above and beyond to surpass visitors' expectations and create unforgettable experiences.

Tailoring services and amenities to your guests' specific needs and preferences, you can improve the guest experience, foster loyalty, and distinguish your B&B in the competitive hospitality industry, resulting in increased guest satisfaction and positive word-of-mouth recommendations.

Chapter 9

Managing visitor comments

Managing visitor comments and reviews is critical for ensuring guest happiness, improving the guest experience, and protecting your bed and breakfast's brand. By actively listening to guest input, resolving complaints, and leveraging favorable evaluations, you may improve your B&B's reputation and attract more visitors.

Here's a full description of how to efficiently manage visitor comments and reviews:

1. Prompt Response: Respond to every visitor's feedback and reviews, favorable or negative. Acknowledge visitors' input and thank them for taking the time to share their ideas and experiences. Respond to reviews within 24-48 hours to demonstrate your dedication to visitor happiness.

2. Active Listening: Actively engage with visitor feedback and reviews to understand their perspectives, issues, and ideas. Pay attention to common themes or reoccurring difficulties raised in reviews to discover opportunities for improvement and address guest complaints ahead of time.

3. Addressing issues: Respond to visitor issues and complaints swiftly and professionally. Apologize for any deficiencies or troubles encountered by visitors, provide remedies or compensation as needed, and take proactive measures to prevent similar problems in the future.

4. Encourage guests to submit constructive feedback by asking specific questions about their experience and accepting recommendations for improvement. Use guest feedback to find areas of strength and potential for improvement in your bed and breakfast's operations and guest services.

5. Respond to visitor feedback and evaluations with professionalism, civility, and empathy. Maintain a cheerful and courteous tone while responding to unfavorable criticism or complaints. Showcase your commitment to visitor satisfaction and your willingness to resolve any issues to the best of your ability.

6. Maximizing Positive Reviews: Highlight and use favorable evaluations as testimonies and recommendations for your B&B's quality and service. Share favorable evaluations on your website, social media platforms, and marketing materials to demonstrate visitor pleasure and attract new customers. Express thanks to guests who give positive feedback and urge them to share their experiences with others.

7. Learning chances: Consider visitor feedback and evaluations as opportunities for continual growth. Analyze feedback patterns, identify areas for improvement, and make the required modifications or upgrades to improve the guest experience and surpass their expectations.

8. Monitoring Review Platforms: Regularly monitor review platforms, travel websites, and social media channels for guest input and reviews of your bed and breakfast. Use online reputation management solutions to track and manage reviews across numerous platforms and respond quickly to guest input.

9. Transparency and Authenticity: Respond transparently and authentically to guest feedback and reviews. Address visitor issues openly, offer honest explanations or solutions, and show your dedication to guest satisfaction and continual growth.

10. Follow-Up and Engagement: Thank visitors for their feedback and assure their pleasure. Use guest feedback to customize future encounters, and connect with visitors proactively to foster long-term relationships and commitment to your bed and breakfast.

Adapting To Industry Developments

Adapting to industry developments is critical to the long-term profitability and viability of your bed and breakfast (B&B) business. As the hospitality business changes, it is critical to be adaptable and proactive in responding to market trends, technological improvements, and shifting guest preferences.

Here's an in-depth look at how to properly adjust to industry changes:

1. Market research and trend analysis: Stay up-to-date on industry trends, market dynamics, and changing guest preferences by doing constant market research and trend analysis. Stay up-to-date on the newest advancements and emerging trends by reading industry publications, attending hospitality conferences, and engaging with industry groups.

2. Foster a flexible and agile culture at your B&B to adapt swiftly and effectively to industry developments. Be willing to adapt your business plans, offers, and processes in response to changing market conditions, guest feedback, and new prospects.

3. **Technology Integration:** Use technology to simplify operations, improve guest experiences, and remain competitive in the digital age. Invest in property management systems (PMS), online booking platforms, mobile applications, and other technological tools to automate procedures, increase productivity, and match guests' needs for seamless digital experiences.

4. Adopt a guest-centric strategy to meet evolving tastes and expectations. Solicit visitor input, listen to their wants and preferences, and modify your offers and services to meet or exceed their expectations.

5. Diversify your B&B's offerings to cater to shifting market demands and attract a wider range of guests. Consider going beyond typical hotel accommodations to include additional

services, facilities, and experiences that cater to various visitor demographics and tastes, such as eating, wellness, event hosting, or outdoor activities.

6. Sustainability Initiatives: Promote eco-friendly practices to meet customer demand for ecologically aware travel. Implement green initiatives like energy-saving measures, trash reduction, recycling programs, and eco-friendly facilities to attract eco-conscious tourists and distinguish your B&B in the market.

7. Collaboration and Partnerships: Work with local companies, attractions, tour operators, and event organizers to adapt to industry changes and improve your B&B's services. Form strategic relationships to generate packaged packages, cross-promotional possibilities, and one-of-a-kind guest experiences that capitalize on your partners' skills and resources.

8. Training and Development: Invest in continual training and development for your personnel to ensure they can adapt to industry changes and provide excellent visitor experiences. To prepare your personnel to meet changing visitor expectations, provide training in customer service, technology use, environmental practices, and industry trends.

9. Continuous Innovation: Create a culture of innovation within your B&B to keep ahead of industry developments and generate growth. Encourage your team's creativity, experimentation, and idea creation to uncover new possibilities, develop novel offerings, and differentiate your bed and breakfast in a competitive market landscape.

10. Monitoring and Evaluation: Constantly monitor industry trends, guest comments, rival activity, and market dynamics to assess the efficacy of your plans and make adjustments as needed. Review and adapt your business goals, marketing tactics, and operational methods on a regular basis to keep current with industry trends and optimize prospects for success.

Proactively responding to market changes, embracing innovation, and putting guest pleasure first, you can position your bed and breakfast for long-term success and sustainability in the dynamic and competitive hospitality sector.

Embracing technology in bed and breakfast operations

Embracing technology in bed and breakfast operations is critical for increasing productivity, improving guest experiences, and remaining competitive in the hospitality business. By embracing cutting-edge technology, B&B operators may streamline operations, improve guest services, and attract tech-savvy customers.

Here's a full explanation of how to incorporate technology in bed and breakfast operations:

1. Online booking and reservation systems: Set up an online booking and reservation system that lets customers reserve rooms directly from your website or mobile app. To speed up the booking process and increase visitor convenience, employ a user-friendly booking platform that provides real-time availability, secure payment processing, and automatic confirmation emails.

2. Property Management System (PMS): Consider investing in a cloud-based property management system (PMS) that includes reservations, guest check-in/out, house-keeping

scheduling, and invoicing capabilities. A project management system (PMS) allows you to consolidate operations, automate administrative processes, and access real-time data to make better choices and increase efficiency.

3. Mobile Applications and Self-Service Solutions: Create a smartphone application or install self-service kiosks in your B&B to improve visitor interactions and expedite service delivery. Allow customers to check in online, access room keys digitally, request amenities or services, and submit feedback via mobile applications or self-service portals, which will increase convenience and reduce wait times.

4. Contactless Check-In and Keyless Entry: Provide contactless check-in and keyless entry systems, allowing guests to skip the front desk and enter their rooms using mobile devices or electronic key cards. Implementing contactless technology increases safety and efficiency, as well as giving passengers a more seamless arrival experience.

5. Use guest experience management platforms or CRM systems to gather preferences, track interactions, and tailor experiences. Collect visitor feedback using automated

surveys or guest reviews included in your PMS to identify areas for improvement and increase guest satisfaction.

6. High-Speed Internet and In-Room Technology: Provide current technological conveniences in guest rooms, such as smart TVs, streaming services, Bluetooth speakers, and charging stations. To ensure consistent Wi-Fi coverage across your property to fulfill the connection requirements of tech-savvy visitors and improve their overall experience.

7. Online marketing and digital presence: To increase exposure and attract tourists, establish a strong online presence by creating a professional website, active social media accounts, and using online travel agents. Use digital marketing tactics like search engine optimization (SEO), pay-per-click (PPC) advertising, and email marketing to target potential visitors and increase reservations.

8. Revenue Management and Analytics Tools: Use revenue management software and analytics to monitor market trends, rival pricing, and optimize room rates and inventories. For your bed and breakfast, use data-driven insights to estimate demand, dynamically modify pricing strategies, and increase revenue and profitability.

9. Automation and smart home technology: Use automation and smart home technology to improve visitor comfort and streamline operations. Automate processes like temperature management, lighting, and housekeeping scheduling to increase energy and operational efficiency while providing visitors with a tailored and easy experience.

10. Staff Training and Assistance: Offer extensive training and ongoing support to help employees adapt to new technologies and successfully use them in everyday operations. Ensure that employees are skilled at using software systems, mobile applications, and digital tools to provide flawless guest experiences and fix technological difficulties as needed.

Chapter 10

Addressing Problems

Addressing problems and responding to market trends are critical to the long-term profitability and sustainability of your bed and breakfast (B&B) business. You can overcome challenges, capitalize on emerging possibilities, and stay relevant in a changing industry by remaining proactive, adaptable, and inventive.

Here's a full discussion on how to solve difficulties and adjust to market developments at your bed and breakfast:

1. Conduct frequent market research and analysis to keep current with industry trends, rival strategies, and changing guest preferences. Monitor market trends, economic data, and demographic changes to identify potential difficulties and opportunities for your bed and breakfast.

2. To flexibility and agility in business processes to adjust to changing market conditions and guest demand. Be willing to adapt your offers, services, and marketing methods to

successfully match changing visitor demands and preferences.

3. Guests' Feedback and Adaptation: Solicit feedback from guests via surveys, reviews, and direct conversation to better understand their experiences, preferences, and expectations. Use guest feedback to identify areas for improvement and adjust your bed and breakfast's offerings and services accordingly.

4. Diversify your B&B's offerings to appeal to a wider spectrum of customers and meet shifting market needs. Investigate chances to bring new facilities, packages, or experiences that are consistent with developing trends and appeal to a variety of visitor demographics and interests.

5. Strategic Marketing and Promotion: Create successful methods to reach and engage target audiences in a competitive market. Use digital marketing channels, social media platforms, and targeted advertising campaigns to increase awareness of your bed and breakfast, differentiate your brand, and attract customers.

6. Collaboration and relationships: Form relationships with local companies, attractions, event organizers, or tourism boards to improve your B&B's services and attract more guests. Partnering with comparable firms or engaging in joint campaigns might help you expand your reach and leverage common resources.

7. Continuous Training and Development: Invest in ongoing training and development for yourself and your employees to keep current with industry best practices, new technology, and emerging trends. Equip your staff with the necessary skills and expertise to provide excellent guest experiences and efficiently adjust to shifting market circumstances.

8. Financial Planning and Risk Management: Implement effective risk management techniques to reduce obstacles and provide financial stability for your B&B. Monitor costs, have enough cash on hand, and plan for contingencies to deal with economic downturns or unexpected interruptions.

9. Sustainable practices and adaptation: Adopt sustainable practices and tailor your B&B's operations to meet environmental and social sustainability objectives. Implement eco-friendly initiatives, energy-saving measures,

and responsible tourism practices to appeal to environmentally concerned tourists while also contributing to sustainability efforts.

10. Foster a culture of innovation and distinction to stand out in a competitive market and continuously update your B&B's offers and services. Continue to be innovative, explore new ideas, and differentiate your business by providing unique experiences, customized service, and excellent visitor pleasure.

Addressing problems, remaining adaptive, and responding proactively to market trends can position your bed and breakfast for long-term success and resilience in the ever-changing hospitality sector.

Future Trends and Developments in the Bed And Breakfast Sector

Future trends and developments in the bed and breakfast (B&B) sector are always changing, driven by shifting guest tastes, technology improvements, and growing market dynamics. Staying ahead of these trends is critical for B&B

owners to remain competitive and fulfill the changing expectations of their customers.

Here are some probable future trends and breakthroughs in the bed and breakfast sector.

1 Digital Transformation: The bed-and-breakfast business will continue to evolve digitally, with a focus on online booking platforms, smartphone check-in/out, and digital concierge services. B&Bs will invest in technology to improve the guest experience, streamline operations, and increase efficiency.

2. Personalized Experiences: When staying at a bed and breakfast, guests want a personalized and unique experience. Future trends will center on personalizing services and facilities to particular visitor preferences, utilizing guest data and technology to create tailored experiences that address specific needs and interests.

3. Sustainability and Environmentally Friendly Practices: Sustainability and eco-friendly practices are becoming increasingly important in the hospitality business, especially bed and breakfasts. To attract environmentally concerned visitors, B&Bs will implement sustainable efforts such as energy-efficient architecture, trash reduction, locally produced items, and eco-friendly services.

4. Wellness and Health-Related Offerings: As people's knowledge of health and wellbeing grows, B&Bs will add wellness-focused activities like yoga retreats, meditation sessions, spa treatments, and healthier cuisine alternatives. Guests will seek out B&Bs that promote wellness and provide amenities to help them maintain their physical and emotional well-being.

5. Remote work and pleasure travel: The advent of remote work and flexible lives has resulted in an increase in leisure travel, which combines business and leisure activities. B&Bs will appeal to remote workers and leisure tourists by providing services such as high-speed internet, specialized workplaces, and recreational activities to help them balance work and pleasure.

6. Authentic Experiences and Local Immersion: Guests are increasingly looking for real and engaging experiences that allow them to interact with the local culture, tradition, and community. Future trends will emphasize unique local experiences like farm-to-table meals, cultural seminars, guided tours, and encounters with craftsmen and communities.

7. Contactless and Touchless Technology: In reaction to the COVID-19 epidemic, there is an increased demand for contactless and touchless solutions in the hospitality industry, especially bed and breakfasts. Future developments will include the use of contactless check-in and check-out, keyless entrance systems, smartphone payments, and voice-activated assistants to reduce physical interaction and improve cleanliness.

8. Flexible Booking Policy: To accommodate fluctuating travel plans and uncertainty, B&Bs will need to implement more flexible booking arrangements. Future trends will include flexible cancellation policies, refundable deposits, and the ability to reschedule stays without penalty, giving guests peace of mind and flexibility.

9. Community Engagement and Social Responsibility: B&Bs will become more involved in the local community and embrace social responsibility activities that promote community development, cultural preservation, and social issues. To positively impact the local community, future trends will emphasize collaborations with local companies, nonprofit groups, and community activities.

10. Innovative Design and Architecture B&Bs will experiment with new design concepts and architectural styles to offer distinctive and memorable guest experiences. Future trends might include eco-friendly architecture, modular construction, sustainable materials, and adaptive reuse of old structures to provide unique and visually appealing lodgings.

Business Plan Template

Example business plan template for a bed and breakfast (B&B) business:

[Your Bed & Breakfast Name] Business Plan

1. Executive Summary: Provide an overview of your B&B company concept, including location, unique selling proposition, target market, and revenue estimates.

2. Business Description: Provide an overview of your bed and breakfast business, including your vision, mission statement, values, and goals. Describe the concept, theme, and ambiance of your bed and breakfast.

3. Market Analysis: Examine the B&B industry's trends, size, growth potential, and competitive landscape. Identify your target market, consumer demographics, and main rivals.

4. Marketing and Sales Strategy: Describe your marketing and sales strategy, including branding, web presence, advertising, promotions, and pricing. Outline how you want to attract people and create reservations.

5. Operations Plan: Describe your B&B operations, including facilities, amenities, services, staffing, and guest management. Describe your check-in and checkout processes, housekeeping standards, and guest interactions.

6. Financial Plan: Provide financial predictions for your B&B, including starting costs, operational expenses, revenue forecasts, and break-even analysis. Determine your pricing strategy, occupancy rates, and profit margins.

7. Management and Organization: Provide an overview of your B&B's management structure and organization. Describe the duties and responsibilities of important persons, such as the owner, manager, and employees.

8. Legal and Regulatory Compliance: Understand the legal and regulatory requirements for running a bed and breakfast business, including permits, licenses, zoning restrictions, and health and safety standards.

9. Risk Management: Evaluate the possible risks and challenges of running a bed and breakfast business. Outline your risk mitigation methods, contingency plans, and insurance coverage.

10. Sustainability and Social Responsibility: Describe your bed and breakfast's dedication to sustainability, environmental stewardship, and social responsibility. Describe measures to reduce environmental effects and help the local community.

11. Appendices: Additional supporting papers include floor plans, sample meals, marketing brochures, important staff resumes, and other pertinent information.

Feel free to modify and expand on each component of this template to meet the specific needs and aims of your B&B business. A well-written business plan acts as a road map for success, allowing you to get money, attract investors, and steer your company's growth.

Best of luck with your B&B enterprise!

Legal checklist for bed and breakfast (B&B)

Legal checklist for bed and breakfast (B&B) owners to verify compliance with applicable laws and regulations:

1. Business Structure: Choose an appropriate legal form for your bed and breakfast business, such as a sole proprietorship, partnership, limited liability company (LLC), or corporation. Consider liability protection, tax consequences, and ease of administration.

2. Register your bed and breakfast business with local, state, provincial, and federal authorities. Obtain the licenses, permits, and registrations required to run a hospitality business in your area.

3. Zoning and Land Use: Make sure your land is designated for commercial use, such as operating a bed and breakfast. Check local zoning restrictions and land use legislation to ensure compliance with permitted land use and occupancy criteria.

4. Comply with relevant health and safety rules for hospitality operations, such as food safety, fire safety, building codes, and cleanliness. Obtain the appropriate health department permits and inspections for food service businesses.

5. Licenses and permissions: get the necessary licenses and permissions for running a bed and breakfast, including business, lodging, and alcohol permits (if selling alcohol). Additionally, get health department permits for food service operations.

6. Tax Compliance: Recognize your tax duties as a B&B owner, including income, sales, occupancy, and property taxes. Maintain accurate financial records, file timely tax reports, and follow all relevant tax reporting rules for your firm.

7. Employment Law Compliance: Follow employment rules and regulations regarding hiring, salaries, hours, and workplace safety. Understand employee rights, responsibilities, and benefits, as well as follow labor regulations regarding minimum wage, overtime compensation, and employee categorization (e.g., employee vs. independent contractor).

8. Create guest agreements and regulations for bookings, cancellations, deposits, check-in/out processes, and guest behavior. Ensure that your policies are clear, fair, and in accordance with applicable laws and regulations.

9. Protect your B&B's intellectual property, such as trademarks, copyrights, and trade secrets. Consider registering trademarks for your bed and breakfast's name, logo, and branding aspects to avoid unlawful use by others.

10. Obtain adequate insurance coverage for your bed and breakfast business, such as property, liability, business interruption, and workers' compensation. To determine your insurance requirements and secure appropriate coverage, consult an insurance agent.

11. Accessibility Compliance: Ensure visitors with disabilities follow accessibility laws and regulations. Provide suitable accommodations for disabled guests, such as accessible parking, entrances, and lodgings.

12. Data Protection and Privacy: Implement procedures to secure visitor information and comply with privacy regulations. Securely store visitor data, obtain authorization for data collection and usage, and keep sensitive information safe from unauthorized access or exposure.

13. Create contractual agreements with suppliers, vendors, contractors, and service providers to define terms, duties, and obligations. Review contracts thoroughly and seek legal counsel if necessary to ensure compliance with contractual obligations.

14. Implement dispute resolution methods to address guest complaints, conflicts, and legal difficulties. Create rules and processes for resolving disagreements, handling complaints, and ensuring visitor satisfaction.

15. Regularly monitor compliance with legal and regulatory standards for your B&B business. To ensure continued compliance, maintain awareness of changes in laws and regulations, perform periodic assessments, and revise policies and processes as needed.

Following this legal checklist, bed and breakfast entrepreneurs can reduce legal risks, ensure compliance with applicable laws and regulations, and run their businesses responsibly and ethically. It is best to obtain legal assistance from a knowledgeable attorney to solve particular legal problems and guarantee that your B&B business is fully compliant.

Resource Directory For Bed And Breakfast (B&B) Owners

The following is a resource directory for bed and breakfast (B&B) owners, including associations, suppliers, and support services:

Associations

1. Professional Association of Innkeepers International (PAII): PAII is a prominent association for innkeepers and bed and breakfast owners, providing information, networking opportunities, and educational programs to promote the sector. Website: https://paii.org/.

2. Association of Independent Hospitality Professionals (AIHP): This association supports independent innkeepers and small hotel businesses by providing education, advocacy, and networking opportunities. Website address: https://www.aihp.org/

3. The Bed and Breakfast Association of Kentucky (BBAK): The Kentucky Bed and Breakfast Association offers lobbying, information, and networking opportunities for its members. Website address: https://www.kentuckybb.com/

4. The California Association of Boutique & Breakfast Inns (CABBI) is a California-based organization that promotes boutique inns, bed and breakfasts, and small lodging establishments through marketing, advocacy, and instructional materials. Website address: https://www.cabbi.com/

Suppliers

1. The Hospitality Suppliers Network: A comprehensive online list of hospitality suppliers who provide items and services suited to the needs of bed and breakfast operators,

such as bedding, linens, amenities, furnishings, and more,. Website address: https://www.hospitalitysuppliers.net/

2. InnStyle: A provider of quality linens, bedding, amenities, and other hospitality items geared for B&Bs, inns, and boutique hotels. Website address: https://www.innstyle.com/

3. Guest Supply: A top provider of hospitality products, toiletries, linens, and other guestroom necessities to B&Bs, hotels, and resorts. Website address: https://www.guestsupply.com/

4. Webstaurant Store: An online seller of restaurant and hospitality goods that provides a diverse selection of products such as kitchen equipment, dining supplies, cleaning supplies, and more. Website address: https://www.webstaurantstore.com/

Support Services

1. Bed and Breakfast Consultants: consulting businesses that advise, guide, and support B&B owners on many aspects of operations, marketing, and management.

Example: The B&B Team (website: https://bbteam.com/).

2. Accounting and Financial Services: Accounting companies and financial advisers who specialize in assisting small businesses, including bed and breakfasts, provide services such as bookkeeping, tax preparation, financial planning, and budgeting.

Example: Xero (website: https://www.xero.com/).

3. Hospitality Software Providers: Companies that provide software solutions designed specifically for bed and breakfasts, such as property management systems (PMS), booking engines, channel managers, and guest experience management platforms.

As an example, consider Cloudbeds (https://www.cloudbeds.com/).

4. Marketing and Website Design Services: Marketing agencies and web design businesses that specialize in hospitality marketing, branding, website design, search engine optimization (SEO), and digital marketing strategies for bed and breakfasts.

Example: Acorn Internet Services (website: https://acorn-is.com/).

This resource directory connects B&B owners with groups, suppliers, and support services targeted to their needs, allowing them to network, source items, and seek expert assistance to improve their B&B operations and services.

Terms and Meanings Relating To the Bed And Breakfast (B&B) Industry

The following are essential terms and meanings relating to the bed and breakfast (B&B) industry:

1. Bed and breakfast (B&B) is a form of housing that offers clients individual bedrooms and breakfast. B&Bs provide individualized service and typically offer a more intimate setting than bigger hotels.

2. Hospitality business: The hospitality business encompasses lodging, food and beverage, event planning, and allied areas. Bed and breakfasts are part of the hospitality business.

3. Property Management System (PMS): B&B owners use this software to manage reservations, check-ins, check-outs, room availability, and other operational chores.

4. Occupancy Rate: The percentage of rooms or units occupied in a lodging establishment during a certain period. It is an important statistic for evaluating the performance and efficiency of a bed and breakfast.

5. RevPAR (Revenue per Available Room) is a performance indicator in the hotel and lodging business that calculates revenue per available room. Divide total room income by the number of available rooms to determine it.

6. Booking Engine: An online tool or platform connected with a B&B's website, allowing guests to book rooms directly.

7. Amenities: Additional amenities or services offered by a B&B to improve the visitor experience. This might include Wi-Fi, parking, a free breakfast, and other amenities.

8. Turnkey: A property or company that is ready for immediate usage without major adjustments or setup.

9. Check-In and Check-Out: The procedure of officially starting and ending a guest's stay.

10. Upselling: offering additional services or upgrades to enhance the visitor experience and raise income for the B&B.

11. Commission: A portion of the room rate or income paid to third-party booking platforms, travel agencies, or online travel agents (OTAs) to facilitate reservations.

12. Direct Booking: Reservations made directly with the B&B without the use of third-party platforms. Direct reservations often result in larger profit margins for the hotel.

13. TripAdvisor is an internet platform for tourists to discover and evaluate hotels, including bed and breakfasts. Positive TripAdvisor reviews may have a big influence on a bed and breakfast's reputation.

14. Eco-Friendly or Green B&B: A bed and breakfast that prioritizes sustainable practices, including energy efficiency, waste minimization, and local and organic items.

15. Boutique Inn: A tiny, upmarket accommodation resort with customized service and unique features. Boutique inns may follow a certain theme or design approach.

16. The Net Promoter Score (NPS) is a statistic for measuring customer happiness and loyalty. It is based on the possibility that visitors will recommend the bed and breakfast to others.

17. Local Tourism Board: A government-sponsored body that promotes tourism and supports local businesses, such as bed and breakfasts, in a given region.

Understanding this important terminology will help B&B owners navigate the industry, communicate effectively, and make educated decisions that will improve the guest experience and overall business performance.

www.ingramcontent.com/pod-product-compliance
Lightning Source LLC
Chambersburg PA
CBHW071915210526
45479CB00002B/428